Fundamentals of

Patenting
and
Licensing
for Scientists
and Engineers

Fundamentals of
Patenting and Licensing
for Scientists and Engineers

Matthew Y Ma
Scientific Works, USA

World Scientific

NEW JERSEY · LONDON · SINGAPORE · BEIJING · SHANGHAI · HONG KONG · TAIPEI · CHENNAI

Published by

World Scientific Publishing Co. Pte. Ltd.

5 Toh Tuck Link, Singapore 596224

USA office: 27 Warren Street, Suite 401-402, Hackensack, NJ 07601

UK office: 57 Shelton Street, Covent Garden, London WC2H 9HE

British Library Cataloguing-in-Publication Data
A catalogue record for this book is available from the British Library.

FUNDAMENTALS OF PATENTING AND LICENSING FOR SCIENTISTS AND ENGINEERS

ISBN-13 978-981-283-420-1
ISBN-10 981-283-420-6

Printed in Singapore by World Scientific Printers

To Katherine, Liliana and Margaret

Contents

Foreword

This thoughtfully organized and easy to understand book fills a conspicuous hole in the patent literature directed to engineers and scientists by providing a comprehensive overview of the patent value creation and extraction process. The process typically starts with the solution to a particular technical problem. The solution is then broadened, with the help of patent counsel, into a working definition of a potentially patentable *invention* that may also represent the solution to other problems. The boundaries of the invention definition are negotiated with the applicable national patent office and the result of this dialogue is expressed as a set of precisely delineated claims in one or more issued patents. Finally, the intangible asset value represented by those claims is extracted via an increasing array of patent monetization mechanisms.

It is universally acknowledged that intellectual capital plays a critical role in today's knowledge-based economy. Patents, in particular, represent a carefully crafted legal and societal balance between private and public benefits designed to promote the progress of the "useful arts." This balance involves providing a sufficient economic incentive to stimulate innovation on the one hand, and dissemination of the resulting inventions to the public, which then stimulates additional innovation by others, on the other.

Historically, a patent was viewed as conferring on its owner an exclusionary legal right. This right was exercised, i.e., commercially exploited, in one of two ways: (a) by excluding competitors from the market space represented by the patented product or process (via injunction); or (b) by taxing them for the privilege of participating in that market (via license fees). Of course, a competitor always could opt to "design around" the protected subject matter by developing a non-infringing commercial substitute or improvement, but often at significant cost and with the attendant legal risk of being wrong on the question of infringement. The motivation to design around is another way that the patent laws drive follow-on innovation.

Over the past decade however, the perceived economic value of patents by technology companies, and more recently by financial markets, has undergone a dramatic transformation. Patents are now recognized not merely as a bundle of legal rights to be licensed or enforced, but as an independent commercial asset class, like real estate or corporate securities. This change in perception has spawned a variety of new value extraction models for patents based in part on the creative adaptation of existing models used with more traditional kinds of assets.

This new focus on patent value extraction requires a fresh look at the way that patents are created, acquired, managed and monetized. The market value of a patent asset depends on the quality of the patent as measured by the level of advance over the prior art represented by the underlying invention, by the scope of the patent claims, and ultimately by the current and future commercial markets that are impacted by those claims. In the past, many corporate patent development programs stressed the number of patents obtained each year. The result of this approach is that less than five percent of the patents owned by most technology companies have significant commercial value, with the rest being of little or no value. The recent emergence of a patent marketplace, however, has resulted in a marked shift from quantity to quality. The increased attention on patent quality has also resulted from the changing legal environment which has raised the eligibility bar as regards the level of innovation that is required to satisfy the requirement that an invention must not be obvious to a person of ordinary skill in the relevant art.

While patent quality is the key to patent value, the question is, how does one measure quality, either in a relative or an absolute sense? The current patent trading market is inefficient and immature, due to the lack of transparency and liquidity as compared with real estate or corporate securities. This results from the inherently unique nature of a patented invention, from the lack of publicly available transaction data regarding sales of "comparable" patents, and from the inability to reliable measure patent-related risk.

Financial markets have become very adept at applying "risk discounts" to projected future revenue streams of technology start-ups in order to arrive at a risk-adjusted measure of company value. These risks include, among others, technology risk (the risk that the technology will not work), adoption risk (the risk that even if the technology works, customers will not embrace it) and execution risk (the risk that the management team will not be able to bring the technology to the market).

In the case of the patent market however, reliable methodologies for quantifying risk do not yet exist. These include invalidity risk (the risk that someone will discover prior art not considered during the prosecution of the patent that "anticipates" the claimed invention, or in combination with the references that were considered makes it obvious), claims construction risk (the risk that a court will construe the words in a patent claim so narrowly as to negate infringement), and design-around risk (the risk that competitors will be able to offer non-infringing commercial substitutes for the patented invention by eliminating one or more required claim elements).

Against the backdrop of this complex commercial landscape, it is essential that engineers and scientists who are engaged in the business of innovation have a working knowledge of the legal rules, market forces, monetization mechanisms and IP risks that affect the value of their creations. This book will provide that knowledge.

Ron Laurie
Managing Director
Inflexion Point Strategy, LLC
Palo Alto, California
November 15, 2008

Preface

I was once a research scientist working at a prestigious research laboratory for over 10 years. I had a few dozen publications and numerous granted patents. I had frequently dealt with patent attorneys working on patent applications and thought I had pretty good knowledge about patents. However, it was after my 10th anniversary at the research laboratory that I started struggling with the fact that other than the one or two patents being used in the company's products, all of my other patents were just collecting dust. I began wondering what I would do for the next 10 years, were I to continue.

It was around this time that a patent licensing company approached me with an exciting opportunity. If I had not seen the monetization of my own patents I would definitely have wanted to see how a successful innovation company worked on capitalizing their much bigger assets. And most importantly, I wanted to see the insights on the other side of the fence, i.e. once patents are created, how and what methodologies people are using in monetizing them.

It turned out that my first step into the patent licensing house gave me tremendous experience and exposure to many business and legal perspectives of patents that I would not have learned of as an inventor. Later, a number of high tech giants formed an IP consortium aiming to help its constituents to license patents deemed important to their business, in a way to reduce the risk of patent infringement, thus meeting their defensive needs. I had the opportunity to head up the Consortium's first year technical operation, from which I saw thousands of patents in the marketplace and was able to help acquire a handful of important portfolios for the defensive needs of the Consortium's constituents.

Surprisingly, through my exposure to the patent licensing business, I have made two observations:

1. Most of today's existing patents on the market are not profitable at all. The capital generated from patent sales and licensing actually comes from a small percentage of all the assets in the marketplace.

2. A major cause of most of patents not being utilized is that the claims are not written to their full potentials.

I relate this phenomenon greatly to the deficiency in our innovation creating and patenting processes. People seem to think that once a patent is granted, no matter what claims are finally obtained, a great achievement is accomplished. Also, the involvement of most inventors ceases at an early stage of the patenting process. Inventors simply hand out their patent disclosure and technical reports to the patent attorney and walk away from the rest of the process. The inventor's little involvement in the subsequent patent examination has a hugely adverse effect on the ultimate quality of obtained patents.

I realize that there are countless basics of patents that inventors should know. However, to many researchers dealing with patents, the legal aspects of patents are often a particularly big undertaking. My strong connections to scientists and engineers have motivated me to write this book. I intend very much to help inventors easily acquire basic knowledge about patents and their business and legal perspectives. I also aim to include many insightful tips in all aspects of a patent; such broader view of patents will no doubt benefit inventors by creating better assets.

This book is intended to suit all types of inventors, ones employed in corporations, scientists in academia, even independent inventors. It will also be a good resource for corporate patent managers and intellectual property business leaders.

Acknowledgment

I am indebted to my wife Katherine and my daughters Liliana and Margaret for their love, patience and support throughout the writing of this book. They also acted as my reviewers and editors. Margaret also helped with the typesetting of manuscripts. Without their support and sacrifice this book could not be made possible. I am also thankful to my father Guoyu, a math professor and the author of several books, for his continuous encouragement and suggestions.

I am fortunate to have worked with many outstanding people during my early days into the intellectual property licensing particularly patent attorney Mitch Rosenfeld, Dr. Michael Baker and Dr. Gustavo Paz-Pajult. I am also privileged to have worked with many IP business leaders and legal counsels in high tech companies, as well as IP professionals in intellectual property consulting and brokerage firms worldwide. They have provided me with many fresh perspectives on patents. My gratitude also goes to Mr. Ron Laurie, who has graciously agreed to write the foreword for this book. As a respected leader in the intellectual property field, his insights in the foreword bring priceless knowledge to the readers.

I would also like to thank numerous researchers and also inventors, whose great enthusiasm and support have truly motivated me to write this book. Particularly, I thank Prof. Prabir Bhattacharya, Mr. James Billmaler, Prof. Junichi Kanai, Prof. Ge Wang and Dr. Han Zou for their review of my book proposal and their many suggestions. Finally, I thank all those people who have shown great interests and support during the writing of this book. One of their common questions was: "How's your book coming? I would like to order a copy when it becomes available." I found these types of questions extremely caring and encouraging, helping me stay on track, without which the completion of this book would have been much delayed.

Matthew Ma, Ph.D.
Princeton Jct., New Jersey
October 20, 2008

About the Author

Matthew Y. Ma holds a Ph.D. in electrical and computer engineering from Northeastern University, USA. He also holds a M.S. and B.S., both in electrical and computer engineering from the State University of New York Buffalo and Tsinghua University Beijing, respectively. He has near 20 years industrial experiences. At Panasonic Research Company in the US, where he had over 10 years tenure as a senior scientist and program manager of mobile imaging, Dr. Ma has conducted research as well as developed intellectual property strategies for the company's products. He has also served as IP analyst for IPVALUE Management Inc. and the Director of Patent Strategy and Operations for Allied Security Trust, an intellectual property consortium funded by many large high tech companies worldwide. As the founder of Scientific Works, he has provided consultations of patent strategy and assistance in patent filing for start-up companies and independent inventors.

Dr. Ma is also a registered U.S. patent agent. He is an inventor of dozen US patents and numerous international counterparts including Japanese, Chinese and European patents. He is an author of near 30 international conference and journal articles and co-author of a book titled "Personalization Techniques and Recommender Systems". He is serving on the editorial board of International Journal of Pattern Recognition and Artificial Intelligence. He has been an affiliated professor of Northeastern University, China since 2001, a senior member of IEEE and a member of Intellectual Property Owner's Association (IPO). He can be reached at mattma@ieee.org.

PART 1 The Basics

Chapter 1

Introduction

To many people, patents are associated with intelligence, pride and honor. Being granted a patent is considered a significant achievement. But even though obtaining a patent is certainly a milestone, it is absolutely not the ultimate goal.

Many researchers are not clear on when and why they need to file patents. One professor told me his group had developed a tool for teaching a machine to learn to imitate human's voices and decided to file a patent on his underlying speech technology. I asked him if he had thought about patenting his system including design, user interface etc. He said he thought he should focus on patenting the algorithm because it was the core of the system. Unfortunately, what this professor did not understand is that sometimes an invention on a system or user interface that seems to be trivial and less technical can often end up being a strong patent.

I have also heard stories of some companies filing patents on every single incremental improvement of their technologies because their goal was to create intellectual property (IP) for the company and thus, the number of patents counted. Such a strategy is time consuming, very expensive — and completely unnecessary. These types of examples demonstrate to me that there is much confusion among scientists, engineers, corporations and the general public about the purpose of patents, why and under what circumstances patents should be filed and what goals they should hope to achieve by filing a patent.

The focus of this book is to give scientists and engineers various technical, business and legal perspectives regarding patents and the patenting process, with the ultimate goal of helping them create better and higher quality of patent assets that can be utilized.

This first chapter gives a brief explanation of the patent value chain, followed by an illustration of the scope and organization of this book.

1.1   Ideas to Assets: Patent Value Chain

A global picture of the patent value chain is illustrated in Fig.1.1. This process consists of two major stages: patenting and enforcement. The patenting process is primarily concerned with generating patents while enforcement is about enforcing patents after they have been granted, including technology transfer, licensing and sales.

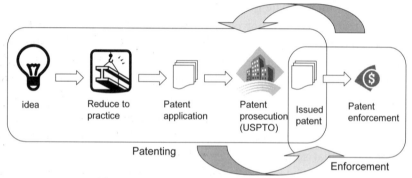

Fig. 1.1 Patent process and patent value chain.

A typical patenting process starts with an idea. This is followed by what is referred to as the reduction to practice. The reduction to practice involves building the invention, experimentation, proving the invention actually works and further refinement of the original concept. The completion of reduction to practice phase is typically marked by the filing of a patent application with the patent and trademark bureau. In the United States, this bureau is the United States Patent and Trademark Office (USPTO), a federal agency under the Department of Commerce.

Under subsequent examination of the application, also called patent prosecution, the USPTO uses laws and rules to examine the patentability of the application. During this process, inventors can rebut and appeal any rejections posted by a patent examiner (often in Office Action). A patent application should not be considered to be a patent unless and until it has actually been granted by the USPTO. Only a granted patent gives its owner legal rights. Only a granted patent can be enforced or licensed.

The enforcement stage is primarily concerned with the monetization of the patent after it is granted. This process is beyond the authority of the USPTO. These two stages of patenting and enforcement happen at different times, and often involve different groups of people. The patenting stage usually involves law firms, patent attorneys and agents who are considered to be part of the patent filing and prosecution system that work all under the guideline of the USPTO. The patent licensing and sales phase will probably involve many business people who are considered to be part of the patent licensing community. The functional division of the patent value chain inevitably causes a disconnection between inventors and the beneficiaries of the invention. Inventors have little knowledge about how their invention is ultimately utilized, whether it is made into a product, licensed, or sold. The main purpose of this book is to fill this information void.

1.2   The Scope and Organization of This Book

This book is not intended to be a "Patent it Yourself" book, nor is it intended to be a patenting guideline text book of the type often written for patent attorneys. This book is intended to help scientists and engineers, whether they are "patent it yourselfers" or people who work with patent attorneys. It is intended to help such inventors turn their technologies into the most valuable assets possible. This book covers various aspects an inventor should know about, from patent preparation to patent licensing, in a language that is easy for technologists to understand.

A unique approach has been taken when selecting the materials and addressing the various topics, differentiating this book from the many similar titles currently on the market. Particularly:

1. Readers of this book are not required to possess prior knowledge about patents or patent laws. If you are new to patents, you will find several introductory chapters which will be quite helpful, and make it easy for you to begin to understand the patent process and the relevant laws. The language used throughout the book can be easily understood by an inventor or technologist without overwhelming him or her with overly complex legal terms and case laws.
2. Patenting and enforcement stages in the patent value chain do not happen in isolation. This book ties the many technical, legal and business aspects of patent enforcement to the innovation and patenting stage. This will give readers much insight into the process of determining whether a patent is strong or weak. It will also show them how to create a strong patent asset.

This book is organized into four parts.

PART I: BASICS (Chapters 1–3)

Chapter 2 discusses some common misconceptions about patents. This chapter will provide you with insightful and valuable perspectives on many common issues inventors frequently encounter, such as exclusive rights, trade secrets, best mode, patent maturity, etc.

Chapter 3 is intended to give the reader a condensed version of patent laws and rules, highlighting all the necessary basic information an inventor will need to know. This chapter may either be read at your leisure or may be used as a reference when any issues arise from your real patenting case.

PART II: FUNDAMENTALS IN PATENTING (Chapters 4–7)

This part covers various aspects of patenting, including how to read a patent, how to harvest your own innovation and how to file your own patent.

Chapter 4 gives the anatomy of a patent and shows you the essentials of reading patents. It will teach you how to understand embodiments and claims. It will also show you which specific things you need to be looking for when reading someone else's patents for different purposes.

Chapters 5 and 6 cover various topics pertaining to innovation, including harvesting ideas, patent landscaping and strategy, making decisions on filing and preparations necessary before you file your own patent.

Chapter 7 gives many details about patent filing, such as what you need to pay attention to in your patent specification, as well as the pitfalls to avoid when working with attorneys.

PART III: PATENT PROSECUTION AND POST GRANTING (Chapters 8–10)

Even most inventors who have successfully obtained patents have little or no exposure to the patent prosecution process since most matters related to this process have probably been handled by their attorneys. Once a patent application has been filed, the inventor is often kept out of the loop in regard to the status of the application. However, there are many important things an inventor should know as he carries out his duty throughout the life of the patent.

The first half of Part III gives many insights on the patent prosecution process and offers practical suggestions about how an inventor should get involved in this process to create a stronger portfolio, all from a real inventor's perspective. Later, in Chapter 10, outlines are also provided for how an inventor should continue carrying out his duty in maintaining the integrity of his invention even after the patent has been granted.

PART IV: BUSINESS PERSPECTIVES AND BEYOND (Chapters 11–15)

Part IV is intended to give interested readers a broad spectrum of business and financial perspectives concerning patents and the patenting process, particularly their monetization. It discusses various issues and common practices in patent strategy, licensing, sales, evaluation, maintenance and valuation. It also highlights some patent database tools and resources to help readers accomplish various tasks pertaining to patents.

What makes this book valuable to scientists, engineers and research managers responsible for creating and managing a company's IP asset is its abundance of insights into various business and financial interests concerning patents. This book gives readers a broader view of what the global intellectual property market is and in turn helps them create stronger patents.

Chapter 2

Common Misconceptions About Patents

This chapter attempts to clarify some common misconceptions about patents often held by many inventors, scientists and engineers. It also serves as an introduction to patent basics for readers who are new to the subject.

2.1 Exclusive Right

2.1.1 *What is Exclusive Right?*

For the last two hundred years, the basic role of the United States Patent and Trademark Office (USPTO) has remained the same, i.e. to carry the duty of the Congress "to promote the progress of science and the useful arts by securing for limited times to authors and inventors the exclusive right to their respective writings and discoveries."[1] Exclusive right gives you the right to exclude others from implementing your invention but does not guarantee that you can make a product based on your patent.

As stated in the patent law, "Every patent shall contain a short title of the invention and a grant to the patentee, his heirs or assigns, of the right to *exclude* others from making, using, offering for sale, or selling the invention throughout the United States or importing the invention into the United States, and, if the invention is a process, of the right to *exclude* others from using, offering for sale or selling throughout the

---

[1] Article 1, Section 8 of the United States Constitution.

United States, or importing into the United States, products made by that process, referring to the specification for the particulars thereof."[2]

Furthermore, as stated in the Manual of Patent Examining Procedure (MPEP), "Ownership of the patent does not furnish the owner with the right to make, use, offer for sale, sell, or import the claimed invention because there may be other legal considerations precluding same (e.g. existence of another patent owner with a dominant patent, …)."[3]

2.1.2   *Exclusive Right and Infringement*

Many people naturally assume it is safe to make and sell products once a patent is granted. This is a misconception. The exclusive right you gain from obtaining your patent is not about what you can do, but rather what other people cannot do. This right only allows you to exclude other people from making products based on your invention. Whether or not you can make your own patented invention depends on whether your product rides on (or infringes) other people's inventions.

A simple test formula for determining whether your product infringes upon someone else's patent is to test whether your product has all the features described in their patented claim. As illustrated in Fig. 2.1, a system claim comprises of 3 components: A, B and C. If Product X only needs A and C to work, it does not have all the features in the patent claim; therefore, it is not covered by the patent claim, and it is not

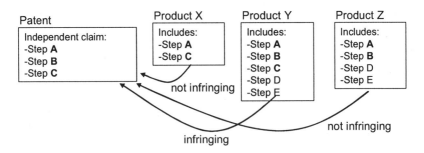

Fig. 2.1 Infringement test

---

[2] 35 USC 154 (a)(1).

[3] MPEP 301.I.

infringing. If Product Y needs A, B, C, and additionally D and E, it has every element in the patent claim (i.e. A, B and C); therefore, it is infringing. Product Z is not infringing because it is missing Step C.

2.1.3   *Infringement and Patentability*

An interesting question is whether it is still possible for someone to obtain a patent with A, B, C, and D and E if a first patent already had A, B and C in its claim. The answer is yes. Infringement of a patent only applies to products, not patents. A patent cannot infringe another patent. If two patents are both claiming the *same* invention, only one can be granted and appeal for.interference must be filed. However, if the claims of one patent are broader than those of the other patent, both patents can still co-exist.

In our above example, if the second patent passes all novelty and nonobviousness criteria[4] usually applied by a patent examiner, it can be granted with claims A, B, C, and D and E. Whether one patent will make another patent nonobvious or nonnovel is the concern of the USPTO, but whether one patent's claims are broader than the other or whether a patent is infringed upon by a product is not the concern of the USPTO.

Another question is: Even if my patent with A, B, C, and D and E is allowed, can I still be prevented from making my own product because it is going to infringe someone's patent claiming A, B and C? If so, then why should I file my own patent in the first place?

Fig. 2.2 Traditional telephone and its significant improvement.

---

[4] The novelty and nonobviousness are basic elements of determining patentability of an invention. They will be discussed in detail throughout the book.

To answer this question, let us take a look at the example shown in Fig. 2.2. In this scenario, imagine that a first patent on a traditional telephone has already been granted. Subsequently, your invention makes a significant improvement by adding a speaker on the phone to enable a hands-free feature. If you make a speaker phone based on your invention, you will infringe upon the first invention because your product will still have all the features described in the first patent's claim — i.e. the traditional phone.

On the other hand, because your speaker phone represents such a significant improvement over the conventional telephone, a possible scenario might be that the owners of the traditional telephone patent and you will negotiate and reach a cross-licensing deal. As a result, you will both be manufacturing traditional and speaker phones. Consequently, competition for better phones and advancement of new technologies will occur.

When you file your patent and intend to launch a product, you will need to do some research and decide if it is safe to make your product without riding on other people's exclusive rights. This type of research is called product clearance or freedom of operation. If you do not do your research, and your product becomes successful, people will surely knock on your door. For many large operating companies, even though they already have a strong portfolio of their own, they still conduct product clearance before any new products are released. As a practical matter, this approach may not be feasible for small firms due to their limited resources.

2.2 A Single Patent Protection Scheme

Some inventors rely on a single invention to make tons of money because they think it is a great innovation or breakthrough. Large corporations however, often have the most advantage in getting larger protection via higher quantity filings.

Figure 2.3 illustrates the common pyramid patent portfolio strategy, and how small companies or universities should balance the variety of their portfolio due to limited resources. This pyramid clearly shows that the combination of different levels of innovations (in terms of broadness of technologies) gives the strongest protection against competitors. It takes many more resources to attack a portfolio with multiple facets than one with a single patent. Moreover, the combination of different levels of innovations gives a better mixture of exclusive rights than a single patent does, and the bundling of a patent portfolio is often part of the strategy for patent licensing and sales, as will be discussed in Chapter 13.

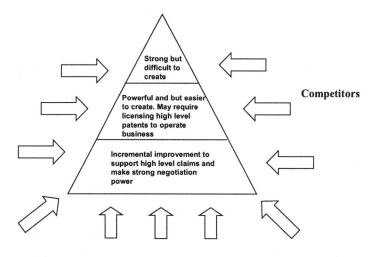

Fig. 2.3 Patent portfolio management strategy.

2.3 Trade Secret vs. Patenting

In a patent application, an inventor is required to disclose explicitly and precisely how the invention works as well as the preferred design. This requirement discourages many people as it appears to be giving up their trade secrets. The questions that most often arise are, "Why should I file a patent since by doing so I will reveal all my secrets? How does revealing my secrets protect my product? Should I patent it or just keep it secret?"

The first question you should ask yourself is how strong your trade secret is, and if there are other ways around it. The downside of keeping an innovation as trade secret is that having trade secret gives you no legal protection [5]. If someone independently figures out your secret or discovers an alternative way of making the same product as yours, you have no way to collect your royalty from them because you have no protection for your technology.

The considerations you will have to take into account are how much longer you can enjoy your market share from your trade secret and the profits flowing from it before someone else figures it out or finds a way to work around it. On the other hand, how much profit can you make in the near term future by patenting your technology and licensing to other people? In the highly competitive and rapidly growing high tech arena, chances are that fairly soon, someone will either come up with an alternative to your secret or market products superior to yours. It is virtually impossible to dominant the market for any length of time with only a trade secret.

Furthermore, a general principle of Patent Law maintains that a first inventor may lose priority if he is deemed to have "abandoned, suppressed, or concealed" the invention[6]. Numerous case laws cover the scenario in which a first inventor has withheld a technology by maintaining it as a trade secret while someone else subsequently and independently invented the same technology and was granted a patent covering it. In such cases, the first inventor has typically learned of the second inventor's patent and took the action of filing a patent application and claiming the early priority date as being the first inventor. In many such cases, "the court declined to award priority to the first inventor. The second inventor, who made efforts to disclose the technology, acted consistently with sound patent policy."[7]

Should companies try to avoid keeping trade secrets? The answer is certainly no. How to decide what to keep as a trade secret and what to file as a patent would take us far beyond the scope of this book.

---

[5] Trade Secret Act does provide some protection with respect to its secrecy and confidentiality perspective.

[6] 35 U.S.C. 102(g).

[7] R. Schechter and J. Thomas, "Principles of Patent Law", Second Edition, Thomson West, 2004.

However, from a patenting and licensing point of view, unless you really think the trade secret can sustain itself for a long period of time and is vital to the success of your business, patenting will ordinarily give you all the protection you need.

The patent system gives you several vehicles to patent your technology without immediately publishing your secrets:

1. <u>Provisional filing</u>. The provisional filing gives you the priority date the same date you file it, yet the provisional application will not be examined nor will it be published as other regular patent applications. The public will have no access to your provisional application. Inventors have up to 1 year to file a regular patent application (called nonprovisional application) from the date the provisional application is filed and can still claim the benefit of early priority date of the provisional. If you are making products and are not sure whether or not to disclose your technology to the public, provisional application is a good vehicle. It allows you to test the market acceptance of your product and later decide whether you want to spend the money and efforts to file and disclose your invention.

2. <u>Eighteen-month publication</u>. Once a patent is filed nonprovisionally, the USPTO automatically publishes the application after 18 months. Until then, the content of your patent application will not be accessible to the public.

3. <u>Request for nonpatent publication</u>. Although the publication of your application is a free tool from the USPTO to advertise your technology, you can request nonpublication at the time your nonprovisional is filed for a reasonable fee. This gives you a substantial amount of extra time to keep your innovation from being accessible to the public. The requirement is that if you decide later to file a foreign application based on your U.S. patent, you need to withdraw your nonpublication request then from the USPTO.

In summary, there are many considerations you need to take into account when deciding whether or not to keep your innovation as a trade secret. Even if you decide to file a patent, the patent system provides several tools that can prolong the period before your innovation has to be exposed to the public. These tools may serve the same purpose as keeping a trade secret.

Do you still want to keep your technology as a trade secret?

A contrary extreme situation to trade secret involves IBM's new policy initiative announced in October 2006, aiming to help improve the patent system. The initiative sets IBM as an exemplar of openness, of which relevant key steps are:

1. Opening more than 100 of its business method patents (representing approximately 50 percent of IBM's total business method patents) to the public for open use, while reducing future business method filings to only those with substantial technical content.
2. Promptly and publicly recording the assignment of all patents and published patent applications it owns.

Clearly, IBM is not shy about letting the public know about its inventions. IBM's actions are not simply giving up trade secrets. Rather, their ulterior motive is to claim the space of its innovations. A market effect of IBM's open policy is that people independently developing technologies similar to IBM's may discover IBM's published applications and quickly abandon their own development efforts. Such independent developers know they would be at a severe disadvantage in a competition due to IBM's already well established position in the marketplace, and will therefore not wish to waste their efforts.

2.4   Patents vs. Publications

There seem to be many questions regarding patents and research papers (publications), especially from those coming from an industrial research environment. Should I publish a paper or file a patent? Should the granting of a patent count as a metric in assessing research achievement? The questions seem to be endless.

Before we attempt to answer these questions, let us make a simple comparison. Table 2.1 shows a comparison of key metrics applied to the review of a submitted research paper and a patent application.

Table 2.1 Metrics for evaluating a publication submission and patent application.

Metrics	Publications	Patents
Relevancy	Relevancy to the conference theme or paper scope	practical/useful
Nonpublish	Not published elsewhere	No double patenting
Novelty	Novel/survey/experiments	Novel
Technical correctness	Technically correct	Enablement
Presentation	Readability, organization, appropriate length	Comply with spec requirement in patent rule, drawings, specs supporting claims
Originality	Original work	Nonobvious against prior arts
Previous work used against novelty	Based on the knowledge of reviewers (total 2–3 reviewers)	Extensive search by the patent examiner over entire patent database and prior conf/journal publications[8]
Economics	Readers' interest	not considered
Examination period	2–3 months with no rebuttal	2–3 years with rebuttal but can be costly

The following observations can be made:

1. It can be seen that the metrics used in the reviewing processes of patents and papers are somewhat parallel. However, there are differences. For instance, the previous work that is considered in the review of a paper for publication is quite different than the previous material considered when reviewing a patent application. For a patent examination, the patent examiner searches through all available granted patents or published patent applications and conference/ journal publications worldwide to determine whether the innovation is novel and nonobvious. The publication reviewing process does not involve such an extensive search of previous papers, and the judging

---

[8] USPTO launched a peer review pilot in 2007 in collaboration with a non-USPTO group for the purpose of enhancing the finding of prior art for the examination of patent applications. More details can be referred to USPTO web site at http://www.uspto.gov.

of novelty depends on the knowledge of individual reviewer, or at most a total of 2 or 3 reviewers.

2. From what might be considered an economic point of view, the decision to accept or reject a paper has to do with the level of interest among mainstream readers, whereas such considerations have relatively little to do with the granting of a patent. Patenting by nature has a strong economic motivation behind it, yet this particular economic aspect does not play a role in the examination process.

Should I Patent My Work or Publish It?

Patenting and publication are intended to accomplish different objectives and final goals:

1. The main purpose of publishing a paper is to show your intelligence. Publication is a means of free information exchange without any strings attached. All publications are considered public information and hence, can be freely utilized by all.
2. Patenting is intended as a method to allow a person to rightfully claim specific information as their own property. In a sense, a patent is also a method of free information exchange (through patent database), but only after the rights of the inventor have been secured via the USPTO filing. Furthermore, the free patent information clearly declares inventors' rights through its claims, and no one can implement the invention claimed by any patents without seeking permission from its patent holders.

To answer the question as to whether you should publish or patent, a few high level considerations should be taken into account:

1. Consider whether a work can be published (as a research paper) or patented, or both. There are limitations on patentable matters[9], for example, theories cannot be patented. The traditional view of utility

---

[9] This will be discussed in detail in Chapter 3.

patents[10] used to concern only hardware, mechanics and tangible items. It has only been recently that people have become aware of the possibility that software and business methods might also be considered patentable items. Even today there are many controversial discussions around this topic. A seemingly trivial idea may not be appealing for publication, but under at least some circumstances it might be the focal point of a powerful patent. On the other hand, a testing and evaluation of various systems for a particular task might be more suitable for publishing as a paper even though such information cannot serve as the basis for a patent.

2. Suppose the nature of the work is suitable for both publication and patenting. Some companies, particularly corporate R&D centers, tend to follow what is referred to as a 1-1 pattern, in which they file a patent and then subsequently publish the information. Strategically, the decision of patenting and publishing a paper should be looked at from a different angle. The consideration of patenting should be focused on the long term economic value of the invention. More specifically, the decision to file a patent should be based on the exclusive right it pertains to, the protection of any existing products it provides, and any perceivable potential application it has to other areas. The consideration of filing paper, on the other hand, should be focused on what kind of audience (academic community) you would like to reach through the presentation of your work.

2.5 Best Mode vs. Protection

Best mode, i.e. the best mode of operation contemplated by the inventor to implement his or her invention, by law, must be disclosed in the description (specification) of the patent application[11]. Basically, this rule

---

[10] Other types of patents include design patents (related to form factor), and plant patents, which are not the focus of this book.

[11] Patent Law 35 USC 112: The [patent] specification shall contain a written description of the invention, and of the manner and process of making and using it, in such full, clear, concise and exact terms as to enable any person skilled in the art to which it pertains, or with which it is most nearly connected, to make and use the same, and shall set forth the best mode contemplated by the inventor of carrying out his invention.

says that if you file a patent, to your best knowledge at the time of filing, you must provide enough details on how your invention works so that other people can build your system based on your specifications.

There is really nothing mysterious about this part of the process. As we discussed earlier, you have come this far and decided to file a patent on your invention rather than keeping it as a trade secret. But how does the patent give you protection? The simple answer is that your protection is not what you disclose in your specifications but rather what claims and subsequent exclusive right you receive as the result of patent examination process.

An invention disclosed in its best mode gives a strong foundation for its claims. An invention not disclosed in its best mode at the time of filing will weaken the validity of a patent. Best mode will be discussed in more detail in Chapters 3 and 7.

2.6   A First Glance at Attorney's Draft

Very often an inventor works with a patent attorney or patent agent who handles patent filing and subsequent patent prosecution. An inventor usually delivers a sketch of the invention, lab notes, or a detailed technical report to an agent and the agent typically comes back with a draft of the specification and claims. At their first glance at the agent's draft, many inventors question whether the described invention is their own. You may be overwhelmed by many new terminologies and strange language.

Don't panic! This is a common initial reaction, but it is not necessarily a problem.

When faced with this dilemma, first, you have to understand where the patent attorney or agent is coming from. Patent attorneys and patent agents are not technical writers who help you write a dressy technical report or polish your existing report. Their job is to help you file your patent with the USPTO in order to claim your legal rights in the best and strongest way possible. They need to understand your invention from technical perspective, and write up the patent specification in a way that conforms as rigorously as possible to the requirements of patent laws.

Most importantly, based on their understanding of your invention, its limitations and potential, they write their description of the claims in the manner they believe will give you and your invention the best protection possible.

The official demands of this goal often requires them to describe your invention in a very formalized technical language and in a legalistic style that may at first strike you as a bit arcane and difficult to understand. It is nothing to worry about, for they know what they are doing. After they have explained it to you, it will begin to make sense.

How to work with an attorney or agent will be discussed in a later chapter. In a nutshell, what you will be getting from the agent and your corresponding actions are listed in Table 2.2.

Table 2.2 Your responsibilities in working with an attorney and agent.

What's returned from attorney/agent	Your action
Patent disclosure form and other necessary forms	Check the accuracy of inventorship
Specification	Check technical accuracies, figures and labels (including added figures by attorney)
Claims	Make a first try to picture what each independent claim is describing, and engage with attorney/agent to understand their strategy when drafting the claims

At point, I would like to make two additional recommendations:

1. Pay great attention to the accuracy of the specification. Also make sure you have sufficient enablement (supporting details) in your invention. Once a specification is finalized and the patent application submitted, the specification cannot be changed. If you attempt to do so, this will be considered new matter and greatly complicate the process.
2. You do not have to know how to write a claim, but please do yourself a favor by trying to understand the claim structure and what each independent claim is describing. Claim structure will be discussed in Chapter 4. Also, talking with your drafting attorney/agent and asking questions is the best method of getting yourself educated.

2.7   Patent Maturity Date

A practical question has often been asked: "My patent is already 5 years old and it is still sitting there collecting dust. How long should I wait before it generates true values?"

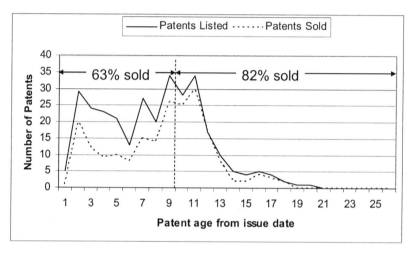

Fig. 2.4 Patent age distribution for Ocean Tomo Spring/Summer'08 Auctions combined.

People like things that are fresh and new: fresh new books, a newly published paper, new technologies and new products. Even in the popular patent benchmarking (for measuring the quality of a company's patent portfolio), the impact factor of a patent[12] retrieves the number of citations only in the past 5 years — to reflect the impact of the technology described within the invention. Indeed, a fresh new patent may be more reflective of the newest technologies and may be indicative of bigger impact on the innovation side.

On the economic side, however, a patent's value may not be apparent when the patent is relatively new. In view of the statistics on Ocean

---

[12] Technical Review defines current impact index (CII) as a measure that showcases the broader significance of a company's patents by examining how often its U.S. patents from the previous five years are cited as "prior art" in the current year's batch.

Tomo public patent auction, Fig. 2.4 shows the age distribution among patents listed on the auctions of Spring 2008 and Summer 2008 combined. The patents covered under Ocean Tomo auction are mainly in high tech areas, with a few in automotive and aerospace. As seen in Fig. 2.4, the percentage of listed patents that have been sold in the older age group (10–20 years) is approximately 30% higher than those within the younger age group (<10 years). The average/mean age for listed patents and sold patents are 7.49/7.0 and 8.41/8.0 years from their issue dates, respectively[13]. Therefore, the patents sold in these two auctions are in average 1 year older than patents that have been listed.

On a larger scale statistics, Fig. 2.5 shows the age distribution among patents listed on the private market for sale[14] in the high tech area from mid-2007 to mid-2008. Among these patents for sale, the average patent age is 7.57 years from the date of issue, which agrees with the Ocean Tomo auction data above, i.e. 7.49 years. The data for private sales is limited only to the patents listed on the market as it is almost impossible to collect any information about patents sold in the private market.

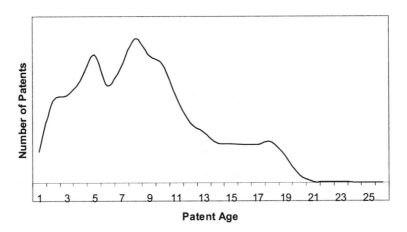

Fig. 2.5 Patent age distribution for 2007–2008 twelve-month private sales.

---

[13] For simplicity, the ages for patents listed and sold are both relative to the year of the auction.

[14] Only United States issued patents were included in the statistics.

In another statistical study[15], it is reported that a patent is typically five years old (from its issuance date) when litigated. This average age is higher for electrical patents, for which the first time a patent gets litigated is closer to seven years.

In view of all above statistics, we may observe that, on average, people attempt to monetize a patent via either sales or litigation when the patent is between seven and seven and a half years old.

The economic value of a patent often has to do with the market acceptance of the invention. This is when a patent matures. Most of the time when a patent is just issued, it may still be too early for the market (no one is using it yet). After some time has passed, an innovation may start gaining market acceptance as the patent matures.

The maturity date of a patent may vary depending on which realm of technology it lies within. If we assume that Ocean Tomo data represents the high tech market, the maturity date for high tech patents is estimated to be around eight to eight and half years from the time the patent is issued. This date is translated to an average of 11–11 ½ years from the patent's filing date.

One form of monetization not included in the previous statistics is patent licensing, specifically technology transfer licensing for which patent is being licensed by the licensee to explore or deploy in the market. Therefore, the technology transfer licensing can happen earlier because it usually occurs before the invented technology is actually used in the market.

How long should you wait for your patent to mature? When exactly you can expect your patent to truly generate value depends on its market acceptance. You should periodically evaluate your patent against the market trend. If the market is heading in the direction of your invention, continue promoting your innovation, and realize that your patent may mature later than average and wait for the time to come. If the market is moving away from your invention, be practical and think of stopping to maintain your patent.

---

[15] Benjamin Hershkowitz, "What Are My Chances? From Idea Through Litigation", http://library.findlaw.com , 2003.

Statistically, a high percentage of patents (e.g. 44% of all patents in computer category), even a majority in some fields (e.g. 74% of patents in golf clubs/equipment category) have expired due to their owners' failure to pay maintenance fees prior to full term[16] (patent maintenance considerations will be elaborated in Chapter 12). You should recognize this fact and not waste any more money on your invention should the market trend so indicate.

[16] James Malackowski and Jonathan A. Barney, "What Is Patent Quality? — A Merchant Banc's Perspective", Colloquium on a Comprehensive Approach to Patent Quality Federation Internationale Des Conseils En propriete Industrielle, Amsterdam, June 8–9, 2007.

Chapter 3

What You Should Know About Patent Laws and Rules

Patent laws and rules are extremely important for inventors to know. Any carelessness, misunderstanding or breaking of the law may result in the rejection or invalidation of a patent, even after it has been granted. Obeying laws is the duty of every inventor and is essential for a patent to remain valid should it be put under scrutiny against the law. This chapter gives an overview of the patenting system and a brief summary of patent laws that engineers and scientists should be aware of.

3.1 The System of Patent Laws and Rules

The patenting system, based on the Constitution, includes three major components: Patent Law (35 USC), Patent Rules (37 CFR) and the Manual of Patent Examining Procedure — instructions to patent examiners (MPEP), as shown in Fig. 3.1. These governing bodies form the ground that all patent prosecution procedures at the USPTO must follow.

3.1.1 *Patent Law*

The law relating to patents consists of various sections of Revised Statues of 1874 by the Congress, and it was not until 1953 that patent law was revised and codified into its substantially present form, which is the Title 35 of the United States Code (35 USC). This code, also called Patent Law or Patent Statue, governs all cases in the USPTO.

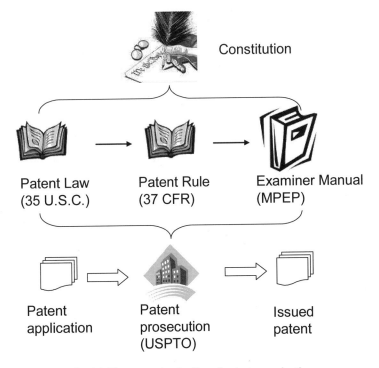

Fig. 3.1 The governing bodies of patent examination.

3.1.2 *Patent Rule*

In 35 U.S.C. 2, it says the USPTO is authorized, subject to the policy direction of the Secretary of Commerce, to establish regulations not inconsistent with law for the conduct of proceedings in the USPTO. These regulations, therefore established by the USPTO in accordance with the statues, is coded 37 CFR[1], and has been used to govern the examiners, applicants, as well as their attorneys and agents.

---

[1] 37 CFR - Code of Federal Regulations, Title 37, Patents, Trademarks, and Copyrights. Parts 1, 3, 4, 5 and 10 of Title 37 are pertaining to patents.

3.1.3   *MPEP*

In practice, in helping with the interpretation of statues and rules and in guiding patent prosecution, the Manual of Patent Examining Procedure (MPEP), as described in its Foreword, provides the USPTO patent examiners, applicants, attorneys, agents and representatives of applicants with a reference work on the practices and procedures relative to the prosecution of patent applications before the USPTO. The MPEP contains instructions to examiners as well as other material concerning information and interpretation, and outlines the current procedures which the examiners are required or authorized to follow in appropriate cases in the normal examination of a patent application.

The MPEP was first published in November 1949 and has been revised multiple times to its present Edition 8. It contains 27 chapters with guidelines on specific aspects of patent prosecution with a total of 2200 pages or 3000 pages if counting appendices including Patent Laws, Patent Rules, Patent Cooperation Treaty, Administrative Instructions under the PCT and Paris Convention.

The MPEP is primarily a guideline for patent examiners, patent attorneys and agents. Although it also claims to be a reference work for applicants, as you can imagine, it is certainly impractical for an inventor to digest all the contents of the MPEP. As a scientist or engineer, and a perspective inventor, you may rely on your representatives, attorneys or agents to follow all the guidelines spread out in the MPEP. However, there are certain basic patent laws and rules that you should know. This basic knowledge about patent law will certainly give you an advantage in your inventing process and help you lay a good foundation in subsequent patenting. This chapter is designed to give you a snapshot of highlighted patent laws in a condensed version.

3.2   Types of Patents

There are three different types of patents: Utility, Design and Plant patents. Utility patent protects the way an article is used and works, while a design patent protects the way an article looks[2]. A plant patent protects any distinct and new variety of plant that are asexually reproduced such as cultivated sports, mutants, hybrids and newly found seedlings[3]. This does not include tuber propagated plant or a plant found in an uncultivated state.

For design patent, the look derives from the ornamental appearance for an article and includes the shape/configuration or surface ornamentation applied to the article, or both. Design patent is more about the form factor of an article. Therefore, a drawing is an essential element of a design patent.

While utility and design patents both afford legally separate protection, the utility and ornamental appearance of an article may not be easily divided. Sometimes, both design and utility may be obtained on an article if the article of manufacture in an invention possesses both functional and ornamental characteristics.

Although most of patent laws and rules are equally applied to utility, design, and plant patents, the discussions and examples in this book are limited to utility patents without losing the generality of fundamentals this book is trying to convey. As a matter of fact, most of patents you encounter are utility patents such as chemical composition, machinery, manufacturing process, tools, software, computer graphical user interface, business methods and algorithms etc.

3.3 Patent Dates

There are several dates associated with a patent, the most important of which is the priority date. Table 3.1 gives a quick glance of each date.

The priority date of a patent in examination is often used by the patent examiner to determine the eligibility of a reference prior art that can be cited to make rejections. The patent examiner first determines the priority date of an invention and attempts to search for any relevant reference prior arts before this date.

---

[2] 35 U.S.C. 171.
[3] 35 U.S.C. 161.

Table 3.1 Different dates pertaining to a patent.

Dates	Meaning
Filing date	The date when the application is filed.
Publication date	The date when the patent application is published at the USPTO website and available for public access.
Issue date	The date when a patent is issued – it is also when the patent holder's exclusive right becomes effective. It is also the date when a patent becomes enforceable.
Expiration date	The date when the exclusive right expires, usually 20 years from the filing date or 17 years from the issue date whichever comes later[4]. Failure to pay maintenance fee may also cause a patent to expire. Upon expiration date, the invention is free for public use.
Priority date	Sometimes referred to as the effective filing date. It is often used to determine the eligibility of the prior art, which may prohibit the patent in question from being granted.

3.4   Eligibility of Priority Date

In many cases, the priority date of an invention is simply when the patent application is filed. This is true when someone conceives an invention and files right away as a regular patent application, also called nonprovisional application. An application can claim the benefit of an early priority date with several mechanisms according to the Patent Law:

1.   Provisional application. If a nonprovisional application is filed less than one year from the filing of its provisional application, it will claim the benefit of provisional application filing date.

2.   Foreign application. If a nonprovisional application is filed less than one year from the filing of its first foreign application (for countries participating in Paris Convention, to be explained later in this chapter), it will claim the benefit of its foreign filing date.

3.   Continuation application. If a nonprovisional application is filed based on its parent application while the parent application is still pending, it will claim the benefit of its parent application filing date.

---

[4] Patent law 35 USC 154(a) and (c).

4. Divisional application. Also a special continuation application. If a divisional application is filed based on its parent application while the parent application is still pending, it will claim the benefit of its parent application filing date.

(12) **United States Patent**		(10) **Patent No.:**	**US 7,184,048 B2**
Hunter		(45) **Date of Patent:**	**Feb. 27, 2007**

(54) **SYSTEM AND METHOD FOR GENERATING AN ANIMATABLE CHARACTER**

(75) Inventor: **Kevin L. Hunter**, San Jose, CA (US)

(73) Assignee: **Electric Planet, Inc.**, Seattle, WA (US)

(*) Notice: Subject to any disclaimer, the term of this patent is extended or adjusted under 35 U.S.C. 154(b) by 449 days.

(21) Appl. No.: **10/045,662**

(22) Filed: **Oct. 18, 2001**

(65) **Prior Publication Data**

US 2002/0118198 A1   Aug. 29, 2002

Related U.S. Application Data

(63) Continuation of application No. 09/173,583, filed on Oct. 15, 1998, now Pat. No. 6,384,819.

(60) Provisional application No. 60/062,361, filed on Oct. 15, 1997.

(51) **Int. Cl.**
G06T 13/00   (2006.01)

5,454,043 A	9/1995	Freeman	382/168
5,548,659 A	8/1996	Okamoto	382/107
5,570,113 A	10/1996	Zetts	345/173
5,581,276 A	12/1996	Cipolla et al.	345/156
5,594,469 A	1/1997	Freeman et al.	345/158
5,991,057 A *	11/1999	Goldstein	359/32
6,141,463 A *	10/2000	Covell et al.	382/286
6,384,819 B1 *	5/2002	Hunter	345/418
6,906,713 B2 *	6/2005	Koshiro et al.	345/420

OTHER PUBLICATIONS

Huang, Chung-Lin; Wu, Ming-Shan, "A Model-based Complex Background Gesture Recognition System", 1996 IEEE International Conference on Systems, Man And Cybernetics. Information Intelligence and Systems Part vol. 1 p. 93-98.

* cited by examiner

Primary Examiner—Ulka Chauhan
Assistant Examiner—Roberta Prendergast
(74) *Attorney, Agent, or Firm*—Van Pelt, Yi & James LLP

(57) **ABSTRACT**

A system and method are disclosed for generating an animatable object. A skeleton of the desired character is constructed by the user utilizing various predetermined components. These predetermined components include a various selection of rods and joints. The rods are static components

Fig. 3.2 The face of a patent and priority date.

5. Invention's conceiving date. In many countries, the law goes with first-to-file, i.e. for the same invention, the first filer will be awarded the patent. The person who filed later will lose his patent rights. However, this is not the case with the United States. The U.S. system is first-to-conceive, i.e. whoever conceives the invention first will be awarded the patent. In reality, the filing date of a patent is often later than its date of conception. However, when a patent application or even granted patent is in doubt or interferes with another patent, if evidence of the development of an invention is procured, the priority date can be moved early. More will be discussed in Section 6.1 on how to maintain your record as evidence.

Figure 3.2 shows an example of the face of a U.S. patent, for which the application was filed on October 18, 2001. As described in "Related U.S. Application Data" section, this patent is also a continuation of its parent application and claims the benefits of its parent application filing date, which was October 15, 1998. Furthermore, the parent application was filed as nonprovisional within one year from its provisional filing, which was filed on October 15, 1997. Therefore, the nonprovisional claims the benefit of provisional filing date.

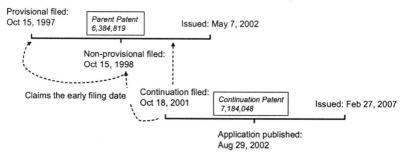

Fig. 3.3 The chain of priority date.

This chain of priority date is further illustrated in Fig. 3.3. Although the patent in the example was filed on October 18, 2001, its priority date was as early as October 15, 1997. The chance of finding relevant prior art before the effective filing date of October 15, 1997 is much smaller than before its actual filing date of October 18, 2001. Therefore, the likelihood of obtaining a patent is higher due to its early priority date. One condition for this scheme to work is that the invention reflected in later claims has to be the same described in early applications. If new matter is introduced and claimed in later applications, this chain continuity of priority date will break.

3.5   Patentability

Many inventors ask how to determine if their invention is patentable before they decide to file a patent. Chapter 2100 of the MPEP has been fully dedicated to this issue. It is also the bible that every examiner follows in determining the patentability of each given patent application. To make it simple to understand the metrics patent examiners are using in making such determination, there are two categories of criteria that will be applied to the patentability test: patentable subject matter and conditions for patentability.

3.5.1 *Patentable Subject Matter*

The fundamental requirement of patentability by law is usefulness. As explained in Patent Law[5], "Whoever invents or discovers any new and useful process, machine, manufacture, or composition of matter, or any new and useful improvement thereof, may obtain a patent therefore, ..." To get the essence of this clause, there are mainly two things to keep in mind in terms of patentability: patentable subject matter and statutory categories of invention test, which will be explained below.

What is Patentable Subject Matter?

The key for any invention to be patentable is that it has to be useful. Whether you are inventing in high tech area, bio-tech, automotive, life science, medicine and plants, almost all the work you have been doing can be useful in a great sense. Therefore, most of the subject matters in your inventing process may be patentable subject matters with two exceptions: abstract useful things and things formed by natural process.

An abstract useful thing means something not indicative of direct use or real-world practical application. A patent has to have tangible, concrete and real use. A computer file in special header and format alone will not be a patentable subject matter unless the new file format is connecting with practical use such as speeding up the reading and writing of files on a media. A state machine diagram alone will not be a patentable subject matter unless its purpose and use are stated. Practically, the statement of intended use or field of use is often clearly stated at the beginning of patent specification.

---

[5] 35 U.S.C. 101 Inventions patentable.

The exception of nature process means any invention needs to be unnaturally engineered. Counter examples are natural phenomenon such as Einstein's relativity theory, Newton's law of gravity, Shannon's information theory etc. Similarly, any plants cultivated naturally are not patentable. Ancient Chinese discovered that certain plants in the wild could cure certain diseases, such discoveries were not inventions. On the other hand, if one has combined several raw materials through a special process to cure a particular disease, it is considered an unnatural manufacturing process; therefore, it is a patentable subject matter.

In recent years, the emergence of software patents and business methods patents have dramatically changed the way people used to think of patentability. The invention is not required to be tangible and concrete in order to be an invention, but its usage has to be concrete and tangible.

<u>Types of Inventions</u>

A popular test for patentable subject matter is to determine whether an invention falls into any of the four types as described in patent laws: process, machine, manufacture and composition of matters. These are also sometimes called statutory categories of invention.

Examples of machine are tangible device consisting of parts, combination of devices, combination of hardware and software all integrated in a tangible hardware device. An MP3 player having a display, memory and software (firmware, audio decoder software, application software) etc. is a machine.

Typical examples of composition of matters are drugs in pharmaceutical industry, special ink composition made for ink-jet printer, chemicals, and man-made materials etc.

Manufacture in its dictionary definition means the production of articles from raw materials by giving to these materials new forms, qualities, properties or combinations whether by hand or by machinery. An example of manufacture includes the production of magnesium alloy material for making rugged laptop case.

Process can be broad. It may refer to a process of making things like special composition of matters. It may also widely cover software methods, algorithms, applications and largely business methods.

This four-category statue has existed since 1836 with the Patent Act of 1836[6] and has been used over and over again in court decisions.

3.5.2   *Conditions for Patentability*

If we cite again Patent Law 35 U.S.C. 101, the complete language reads: "Whoever invents or discovers any new and useful process, machine, manufacture, or composition of matter, or any new and useful improvement thereof, may obtain a patent therefore, <u>subject to the conditions and requirement of this title</u>".

Basically, if your invention passes the patentable subject matter test as discussed in the previous section, it pretty much passed the "usefulness" test. However, it still has to meet various conditions before a patent can be allowed. These conditions and requirements are actually forming the core value of the patent system. In a nutshell, the key conditions and requirements are listed as follows.

<u>Novelty</u>

Novelty is about newness. To obtain a patent, the inventor must create something new. The rule is straightforward: an invention is judged novel unless a single prior art reference discloses every element of the challenged claim and enables one skilled in the art to make the invention. Basically, the key elements in interpreting novelty are prior arts and priority date (to be discussed later).

Very often, an examiner rejects a patent application for lack of novelty by citing a prior art reference that predates the priority date of the application in question. There are numerous topics throughout this book on how priority date is being measured and how to overcome a rejection based on a reference that may have an earlier priority date.

---

[6] The technical change of "art" to its present form "process" was made in 1952.

Nonobviousness

Nonobviousness is about inventiveness. Novelty is complemented by the requirement of nonobviousness. In other words, novelty and nonobviousness are often examined together by a patent examiner. The nonobviousness test is about finding a prior art, upon which the claimed invention is arguably an obvious improvement or an obvious combination of several prior arts from the view of anyone who practices in the same technical field.

The patent examiner often rejects a patent application for its obviousness by citing one or multiple prior arts. In single prior art case, the obviousness may exist based on an obvious variation of the cited prior art. For example, if a prior art describes a table, another invention describing a table with round corners to prevent human objects from being accidentally hit by a table corner may be an obvious variation of the invention in the prior art. Anyone familiar with the table manufacturing may have been able to come up with the round corner variation.

In case of multiple prior arts, the rejection of the claimed invention is based on the obvious combination of two previous works. For example, a copier machine that automatically translates the source English document into a different language is likely rejected based on its obviousness over combination of a copier machine and a document translation system.

Certainly the rejection based on obviousness can be subjective, but once a patent examiner made a rejection based on obviousness, the burden shifts to the inventor to argue about nonobviousness of his invention in the presence of cited prior art(s). Tactics for overcoming rejections particularly novelty and nonobviousness will be covered entirely in Chapter 9.

Other Patentability Requirements

There are other conditions that have to be met in order to obtain a patent. Examples of these requirements are claim support, best mode, claim language etc. These will be covered throughout this book.

3.6   True Inventorship

3.6.1   *Inventorship as Legal Issue*

Patent issuance is based on the presumption that the named inventors are the true and only inventors. This seems to be neglected and has not been made well aware of by many inventors. In writing academic papers, a professor tends to put more than one student's names in his research group on the paper because everyone contributed more or less to the work described in the paper. Similarly in patenting, a technician or summer intern's name appears on the inventor's list because he has helped with the implementation or has conducted necessary experiments. In other cases, a manager's name appears on many inventions made by his team because he leads the team.

The authorship of an academic paper may be more of a business issue. However, the correct inventorship of a patent is a serious legal issue. Although inventorship of a patent is not going to be examined at patent prosecution stage, incorrect inventorship of a granted patent can cause serious legal consequences including invalidation of the patent later should someone challenge at the court.

The law about inventorship as introduced in 1984 is described as: "Inventors may apply for a patent jointly even though (1) they did not physically work together or at the same, (2) each did not make the same type or amount of contribution, or (3) each did not make a contribution to the subject matter of every claim of the patent".[7]

The law does not limit the maximum number of inventors, nor does it require anything about the order of inventors' names or the percentage of contribution in order for someone to be an inventor. In principle, anyone who has contributed to at least one claim should be listed as the inventor. This requirement has loosened much since the 1984 amendment, while prior to 1984, a joint inventor would have to contribute to each of a patent's claims.

---

[7] 35 USC 116.

The law implicitly requires that inventorship is indeed connected with claims allowed and provides mechanisms for correcting inventorship upon rejection of claims. Suppose inventor A contributed to claims 1–5, and inventor B contributed to claims 6–10. Later claims 6–10 are rejected during patent prosecution and the patent was obtained with only claims 1–5 remaining. Then the inventors should file petition to remove inventor B from its inventor's list.

The law does not explicitly specify the nature of the technical contributions that cause an individual to rise to the level of an inventor. However, case laws have shown that an individual must have contributed to the conception of the invention, and furthermore, this person's status as inventor will not be altered even if he rides on someone's services to perfect the invention.

In practice, you should not be too "generous" by adding every relevant person's name to the inventor's list in order to give credits for their work. On the other hand, the law does not limit how many joint inventors can be on the inventor's list; you should not neglect anyone's contribution to the claim even if he contributed to only one claim.

The following case studies give you a better understanding of how inventorship is seriously treated at courts and its consequences.

3.6.2   *Case Studies of Inventorship*

Research Corporation Technologies v. Microsoft (D. Az. 2006)

RCT sued Microsoft for its patents directed to a "blue noise mask" used in halftoning digital images. After the trial, Arizona District Court Judge Manual Real concluded that RCT's patents were unenforceable based on inequitable conduct that occurred during prosecution of the patents in suit. And, because it was an "exceptional case," the judge granted Microsoft's request for US$8 million in attorney fees.

In addition, the judge stated that "Having closely observed both Parker/Mitsa testify, I have been able to evaluate and consider their credibility. In this regard I find that Parker was not credible, and Mitsa was evasive, on many key points in their testimony. This is based, in large part, upon my personal observation of their demeanor while testifying. This lack of credibility and evasiveness of Parker/Mitsa is further demonstrated in Exhibits ... and further supports my above findings on their intent to mislead the Patent Office."

This case law was not much on the correct inventorship. Instead, it illustrates the importance of inventorship. You would want to make sure that everyone on the inventor's list has truly contributed to at least one claim therefore he can withstand a testimony and defend his contributing claim, rather than appearing with no credibility or being evasive about any key technical points.

Ethicon Inc. v. United States Surgical Corp. (Fed. Cir. 1998)

Yoon is a medical doctor and an inventor of numerous patented devices for endoscopic surgery. In 1980, Yoon met Choi, an electronics technician. Choi had worked in the research and development of electronic devices. After Choi had demonstrated to Yoon some of the devices he had developed, Yoon asked Choi to work with him on several projects, including one for safety trocars — a safety device to prevent accidental injury during trocar incisions. Choi was not paid for his work.

In 1982, after collaborating for approximately 18 months, their relationship ended. Choi believed that Yoon found his work unsatisfactory and unlikely to produce any marketable product. For these reasons, Choi withdrew from cooperation with Yoon.

In the same year, however, Yoon filed an application for a patent disclosing various embodiments of a safety trocar. Without informing Choi, Yoon named himself as the sole inventor. In 1985, the Patent and Trademark Office issued the patent to Yoon, with 55 claims. Yoon thereafter granted an exclusive license under this patent to Ethicon. Yoon did not inform Choi of the patent application or issuance.

Later, Ethicon filed suit against U.S. Surgical for infringement of the patent. While this suit was still pending, U.S. Surgical became aware of Choi, and contacted him regarding his involvement in Yoon's safety trocar project. When Choi confirmed his role in the safety trocar project, U.S. Surgical obtained from Choi a "retroactive license" to practice "Choi's trocar related inventions." Under the license, Choi agreed to assist U.S. Surgical in any suit regarding the patent. For its part, U.S.

Surgical agreed to pay Choi contingent on its ultimate ability to continue to practice and market the invention. With the license in hand, U.S. Surgical moved to correct inventorship of the patent claiming that Choi was a co-inventor of claims 23, 33, 46 and 47. Following an extensive hearing, the district court granted U.S. Surgical's motion, finding that Choi had contributed to the subject matter of claims 33 and 47.

U.S. Surgical next moved for dismissal of the infringement suit, arguing that Choi, as a joint owner of the patent, had granted it a valid license under the patent. By its terms, the license purported to grant rights to use the patent extending retroactively back to its issuance. The district court granted U.S. Surgical's motion and dismissed the suit.

In 1998, Ethicon appeals the district court's finding of co-inventorship and its dismissal of the complaint. After the trial, the Federal Circuit affirmed the district court's determination of co-inventorship. What is the ground for this?

In writing opinions of this case, the judge stated: "Taken together, the alleged co-inventor's testimony and the corroborating evidence must show inventorship "by clear and convincing evidence." This requirement is not to be taken lightly." During the trial, in investigating the inventorship of claim 33, the court found Choi's showing of his own sketches similar to the figures in the patent that support the claim in question. Furthermore, the court has discounted Yoon's testimony for lack of credibility and supported the district court's determination that Yoon altered and backdated documents.

Because of the correction of inventorship, i.e. to name Choi as the joint inventor, and retroactive license made by Choi to U.S. Surgical, the patent infringement lawsuit brought by Ethicon to U.S. Surgical were therefore dismissed. This case law is illustrative of the importance of correct inventorship and its legal and business consequences. If Choi was named as the co-inventor at the beginning and perhaps would agree to exclusively license to Ethicon, U.S. Surgical would not have got away with the patent infringement case.

3.6.3 Other Influence of Inventorship

An illustrative example, as shown in Fig. 3.4, is the prosecution history of patent No. 5,666,503, assigned to Xerox. The patent was directed to an image editor and method for editing structured images (SI). At the time the patent was filed, there were two named inventors: Campanelli and Fuss. In the first Office Action, the examiner rejected all the claims based on a prior art: patent No. 5,485,568, issued to inventors Venable, Campanelli, Fuss, Bollman, Nagao, Yamada, and Yamada, and assigned to Xerox and Fuji Xerox. The prior art patent was directed to structured image (SI) format for describing complex color raster images.

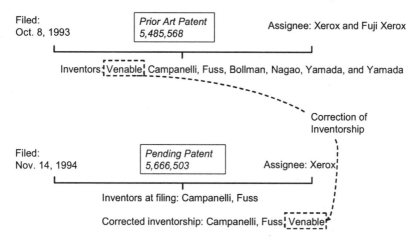

Fig. 3.4 Example of correction of inventorship.

The examiner cited the 5,485,568 patent ('568) and showed that every claim of the pending patent (later issued as 5,666,503) is described in '568 patent, and rejected all claims based on 35 USC 102(e), which reads:

"the invention was described in – (1) an application for patent, published under section 122(b), <u>by another</u> filed in the United States before the invention by the applicant for patent or (2) a patent granted on an application for patent by another filed in the United States before the invention by the application for patent, …"

In order for the rejection to stand, the prior art has to be made "by another", i.e. different inventors. Please note that both the pending patent and the prior art cited by the examiner are assigned to Xerox with common but nonidentical inventors. Xerox has therefore taken a smart step in overcoming the rejection. Instead of arguing about 35 USC 102(e) by arguing technical merits of the invention in comparison to the prior art, Xerox has decided to correct the inventorship with the following two actions:

1. Add Venable to the inventor list of the pending application showing the inventor Venable was missed out without deceptive intention.
2. Declare that Campanelli, Fuss and Venable are the sole inventors of the prior art ('568 patent) in terms of the subject matter disclosed in the pending application.

In this way, as to the subject matter disclosed in the pending application, the inventors for both pending application and prior art are identical, which are Campanelli, Fuss and Venable. This cleared the way to making 102(e) rejection invalid because the prior art has to be made "by another", and in this case it is made by the same group of inventors.

The take home lesson from this case study is that correct inventorship is rather important. An incorrect inventorship may adversely affect your capabilities in patent prosecution or any future patent applications.

3.7   Patent Ownership

Many books talk about patent rights, but few talk about inventors' rights and what inventors are entitled to the inventions they make. This section is giving you a nutshell of the difference between inventorship and ownership and what rights each is entitled to.

3.7.1   *Patent Ownership and Assignment*

First of all, the ownership of a patent is different from its inventorship. Just like any tangible property, a patent has all the attributes of a personal property[8]. As the owner of the property, you do not have to be the original maker. Same applies to patents.

By default, the law states that unless the patent or patent application is transferred and specified in writing, the ownership belongs to the inventors[9]. Whether you work for a corporation, government, university or self employed, you may be wondering, as an inventor, whether you are the owner of the patent or patent application.

If you work for an employer, the ownership of the patent depends on the contract between you and your employer. It is quite common in the United States that you would have to sign an invention agreement with your employer at time of your hire, which agreement states that you agree to assign and transfer and will assign and transfer all your inventions to the employer. Regardless when (within or outside working hours), as long as the invention is within the scope of the employer's business, it is usually covered by this agreement.

Absent any signed invention agreement or contract in that nature with any parties, by law, the inventor is the default owner of the patent.

If you are obligated to assign and transfer the rights of your inventions to your employer, by contract, very often you will be asked to make such transfer in writing at the beginning of the patent application filing. This writing instrument is the so-called assignment form. The assignment form describes the transfer of ownership and will be recorded at the USPTO. Upon issuance of the patent, the name of the current owner will appear in the "assignee" field on the cover page of the patent.

If a patent's ownership is transferred after the patent is issued, such change of ownership will however not be reflected on the cover page of the patent. The ownership transfer post patent issuance is commonly

---

[8] As stated in 35 USC 261 " ... patents shall have the attributes of personal property."

[9] As stated in MPEP 301.I. "... The ownership of the patent (or the application for the patent) initially vests in the named inventors of the invention of the patent." ... "The patent (or patent application) is then assignable by an instrument in writing, and the assignment of the patent, or patent application, transfers to the assignee(s) an alienable (transferable) ownership interest in the patent or application."

recorded with the USPTO, and such record can be publicly accessed via USPTO's Patent Application Information Retrieval (PAIR) system[10].

3.7.2 *Patent Owner's Rights*

As we have discussed before, by exclusive rights, a patent owner does not necessarily have rights to make the claimed invention[11], but he can enforce the patent, i.e. use his exclusive right to preclude others from making the claimed invention. Such enforcement may come in various business practices such as license or litigation. Patent owners have rights to sue their patent infringers or can license their exclusive rights to people who can make their inventions and not be sued.

When it comes to joint owners, there is a misconception that both owners have to agree before a patent can be sold or licensed. Unless there is an agreement on the share of the ownership, by default, each joint owner has equal right and can sell such right without consent of the other[12].

As previously discussed in Federal Circuit case Ethicon, Inc. v. United States Surgical Corp. (Fed. Cir. 1998), the unlisted inventor Choi, who believes he is the true inventor, licensed the patent to United States Surgical without the consent of Yoon. On the other hand, Yoon, the listed inventor licensed the patent to Ethicon. Upon court decision of affirming that Choi is the inventor, such patent has both Ethicon and United States Surgical Corp as licensees and no one can sue either company for practicing the invention.

---

[10] USPTO's PAIR (Patent Application Information Retrieval) system at http://portal. uspto.gov/external/portal/pair. This will be further explained in Chapter 15.

[11] MPEP 301.I. "Ownership of the patent does not furnish the owner with the right to make, use, offer for sale, sell, or import the claimed invention because there may be other legal considerations precluding same (e.g., existence of another patent owner with a dominant patent, ...)."

[12] In patent law 35 USC 262 Joint owners, it says "In the absence of any agreement to the contrary, each of the joint owners of a patent may make, use, offer to sell, or sell the patented invention within the United States, or import the patented invention into the United States, without the consent of and without accounting to the other owners."

3.7.3   *Inventor's Declaration and Rights*

Once you are obligated to give rights of all your inventions to your employer as per your employment agreement, you do not seem to have any significant ownership and power over the patent. True!

On the other hand, many employers offer monetary incentives to their inventors for each patent filed. The amount of money depends on each company's policy, and they usually vary from hundreds of dollars to thousands of dollars. These are much less significant in comparison to what commercial value a patent may generate in the future. But among all the patents a company has, how many patents are usually true money generators? A few percent would be a good number. Plus, if you take into account the cost that has to be paid by the employer to file, prosecute and maintain each patent, the employer bears a lot of up front cost on the other hand.

There are, however, more significant incentives to inventors working at government agencies, universities and government contractors. Inventors at these institutions do not usually have any ownership of a patent, but they may be entitled to the share of royalties from any licensing program based on their invention.

Other than monetary related benefits, inventors play an important role in the inventing and patent prosecution process.

First of all, each inventor is required by law to sign the declaration of invention form to testify that he is the true inventor of the invention. The signing of this form gives inventors both honor and responsibility. There are several other scenarios that inventors' consent is required by law. For example, when filing a reissue patent broadening the scope of claims[13], inventors must sign the oath and declaration form.

In addition, inventors are entitled to being involved in every Office Action on the merit although it is not often the case in practice. This is particularly so when a patent application is handled by a patent attorney, who charges client on production basis with a billable cap. This means that the patent attorney handling the Office Action bills his client by hour with a max limit thus does not often have time to communicate with

---

[13] See Section 10.2.1.

inventors within allowed billable time. In many cases instead, the patent attorney simply responds to Office Action based on his own understanding. The drawback is that very often their arguments turn out to be missing key point of the issue and become unconvincing to the patent examiner.

As an inventor interested in a strong and usable patent, or as a manager interested in the return of investment from innovation of the company, you should make sure there is ample time set for inventors to get involved in the Office Action rebuttal and work with attorneys to come up with the best possible strategy for overcoming any rejections.

3.8   Accelerated Examination

A patent is not really enforceable until it is issued and claims are allowed. As you probably know, USPTO has a huge backlog on patent cases although in recent years they launched initiatives trying to solve the problem by hiring more patent examiners. The typical pending period of a patent application is two to three years, which is the time from when a nonprovisional is filed to when the patent application gets to the hands of the examiner.

If you consider the two-year backlog for each patent case, plus the time needed for Office Action and correspondence, which typically runs about a year depending on the complexity of each case, the total time it takes for a patent to be granted runs from 3 to 5 years.

This creates some economic downside for the patent owner if the patent is intended to protect a product to be launched into the market. However, there are cases under which applicants can file petition to make special, so their application can be taken out of its normal turn — this is also called advancement of examination[14]. The examples of special applications are shown in Table 3.2.

---

[14] 37 CFR 1.102

Table 3.2 Accelerated patent examination.

Special cases	Remarks	Fee required for petition
Manufacture	Prospective manufacture	Yes
Infringement	Actual infringement	Yes
Health	The state of health of the applicant is such that he might not be available to assist in the prosecution of the application if the application were to run its normal course.	No
Age 65	At least one applicant is 65 yrs or older	No
Environmental	Enhance the quality of the environment of human being	No
Energy	Discovery of development of energy resources and utilization and conservation of energy	No
DNA	Safety of research in the field of Recombinant DNA	Yes
Super-conductivity	Superconductivity materials	Yes
Aids/cancer	Advances made in the fields of HIV/AIDS and cancer	Yes
Anti-terrorism	Advances made in the field of anti-terrorism	No
Biotech small entity	Biotech application is a major asset of the small entity and that the development of the innovation will be significantly impaired if examination is delayed	Yes

As can be seen, there are quite a few options available to make your application "special" and advance out of its normal turn. In most cases, the applicant is required to provide either statement stating the reason of petitioning for making special or evidence to warrant each case.

The downside of advanced examination is that for most cases the USPTO poses additional requirements on the application. For example, you will be required to conduct a patent search, which is not required for a normal application. Further, you will need to compare your invention with related prior arts identified in your patent search and present your arguments why your claims should be allowed.

These requirements may be of concern to some people: why would I want to argue myself even before an examiner raises any issues? Why should we not wait and see what if any issues or rejections the examiner has before we present our arguments? From legal perspective, as will be discussed later in this book, any application and prosecution history will be archived and made available to the public through the USPTO's PAIR system. Your arguments, which may be unnecessary, can be discovered by the public and held against yourself in the future.

It is good to know when you are eligible for the advanced examination, but always discuss with your corporate counsel or attorney whether it is the best option for you.

3.9   Enablement and Best Mode

Patent Law requires enablement, i.e. the invention must be operable. In other word, it must be enabled by the process, steps, methods etc. described in the specification. The law also requires the inventors to disclose the best mode in their inventions.

If you look at these two requirements from a different angle, anyone who is a professional in the same field of the invention ought to be able to build and use the described invention based on its specification, and the built system as such shall work in its intended operational mode. In Section 2.5, we have discussed best mode vs. protection. Only if you disclose fully how your system works and its most advantageous implementation based on your best knowledge, can you fulfill your legal requirement. This is indeed compelling inventors to disclose information that might otherwise be maintained as a trade secret.

There are, however, common strategies for fulfilling the enablement and best mode requirement, and at the same time obtaining a broader protection for the invention. Enablement and best mode will taken up further in Chapter 7.

3.10   Patent Search

Patent search is not required by law, although inventors are encouraged to conduct preliminary search to avoid wasteful effort and money later on. If you invent something in the vacuum, you will rely on a patent examiner to do the prior art search and identify if there are any prior art references that are fatal to your patentability. However, it is surely unwise to spend money before even trying to know if something has already been invented that could leave your invention unpatentable.

Before you start writing a patent application to disclose your inventive idea, it is suggested you do a preliminary patent search. The patent search does not have to be exhaustive, but it can give you an intuition what are out there and how relevant they are to your inventive idea. Patent search is a good sniffing test to find out if your invention has already been patented. Another benefit of patent search is that it may give you ideas for alternative embodiments of your invention after reviewing what already exist that may become roadblock for your invention. Chapter 15 will introduce various tools for conducting patent search.

It is worth noting that patent search is not equivalent to product search. If you invent something and find no similar products on the market, it does not mean no one has patented it. The time it takes for a patent to mature and commercialize is typically 5–10 years or longer, depending on the technology and industry. Therefore, new technologies are patented long before you start seeing products on the market. Patent search gives you more insight about technologies and uncovers a greater number of existing inventions than product search does.

3.11 Duty of Disclosure

The duty of disclosure requires inventors or any individual involved to disclose any relevant information they are aware of during patent preparation, filing and prosecution[15].

The reason is reflected in the court opinion cited in MPEP[16]: "[W]e think that it is unfair to the busy examiner, no matter how diligent and well informed he may be, to assume that he retains details of every pending file in his mind when he is reviewing a particular application ...

---

[15] MPEP 2001.06.

[16] MPEP 2001.06 (b).

[T]he applicant has the burden of presenting the examiner with a complete and accurate record to support the allowance of letters patent."

Duty of disclosure does not concern a mandatory patent search. You do not need to dig out information that you do not know. The law says you must disclose what you are aware of and think may be material (critical) to the claims you are seeking. This information may help the examiner determine whether or not your claims are allowable.

Does this mean that you have to observe your competitors patents, possibly killing your own? The short answer is yes. I wish to emphasize the importance of duty of disclosure and the consequence of hiding any key information that you have already become aware of. If you intentionally try to hide critical information from the USPTO, you have broken the patent law and committed inequitable conduct. Your patent can later be invalidated even after it is issued. Your patent should have a strong and solid footing against all the relevant art you know of in the field from the very beginning of the patenting process. Who would you want to spend loads of money for a weak and challengeable patent?

In reality, if you become aware of a piece of key information that may deem all your claims unpatentable, what should you do? You may do one of the two things:

1. If you are convinced that this piece of information is fatal to your invention and there are no claims that can be survived, may be it is your best interest to admit that someone has already invented it and therefore abandon your application entirely.
2. If you still think that some claims (even dependent claims) may survive and you would like to continue pursuing your application even if it may make your claims narrower than originally anticipated, you would need to file an Information Disclosure Statement (IDS) in order to disclose such information to the USPTO.

Finally, the source of information to disclose may include trade shows, communications with any co-workers, competitors, patent infringers or other third parties publications, products, and additionally prior art being cited in related foreign applications, information relating to co-pending US applications, information from related litigation, information relating to claims copied from a patent etc.[17] Examples of information disclosed by inventor will be shown in Chapter 4, and IDS will be further discussed in Chapter 8.

3.12 No New Matter After the Disclosure is Filed

It is important to know that once a patent is filed, there is no new matter that can be added to the disclosure, including the abstract, specification or drawings. Also, no new matter can be added to the claim if there is no support of such matter in the original specification.

Although you may have little room to amend the specification via a correcting procedure after a patent is filed, what exactly can be corrected or added without being considered to introduce new matter is not always clear and may be subjective to the examiner. As an inventor, you should always make your best effort to maintain the accuracy of your disclosure, particularly your specification and drawings at time of filing. Make sure all your claims are well supported in the specification or drawings. More on new matter will be discussed in Chapter 7.

3.13 International Treaty

Each patent granted to you only gives you protection in the country you filed. If you obtain a U.S. patent, it only gives you the exclusive right in U.S. but not in any other countries. Same applies to patents filed in other countries. If you do not have patent rights in a particularly country, yet you are selling products in that country, you run the risk of infringing other people's patents. Therefore, you should file patents in each country you are interested in conducting business. There are two major international treaties to provide you vehicles in gaining protection in foreign countries.

---

[17] MPEP 2002.06.

3.13.1 *Paris Convention*

The Paris Convention, which was formed in 1883, is the foundational and essential international agreement concerning patents. Several original countries include Belgium, Brazil, France, Italy, The Netherland, Portugal, Spain, Switzerland, Tunisia and UK, who entered into force in 1884. Many other countries followed, including the U.S. in 1887, Australia in 1925, Germany in 1903, Canada in 1925, China in 1985, Israel in 1950, Japan in 1889, both North and South Korea in 1980. There are now a total of 172 contracting parties by the end of 2007. This international agreement is administrated by The World Intellectual Property Organization (WIPO), a specialized agency of the United Nations located in Geneva.

The Paris Convention commits its signatories to the following main principles.

<u>National Treatment</u>

Under national treatment principle, a signatory state agrees to treat foreign inventors all equally as domestic inventors in their patent laws, so long as these foreign inventors are nationals of some other signatory state. Examples of treatment are application fees and patent term (life).

<u>Independence of Patents</u>

The independence of patents provides for the independence of different national patents, where each patent in a signatory state is treated independently as in another signatory state. Under this principle, a patentee holding different national patents on the same invention can decide independently, based on its economic viability, which country's patent to be maintained and which country's to lapse, when maintenance fee for each country is due.

Another consequence of independence of patents principle is that patents must be enforced individually in each country. One patent may be enforceable in one country while it may be invalidated successfully by competitors in another country.

International Priority

The most important benefit of Paris Convention is that a patent application filed in one country has the same effect as if it had been filed in another country. The Paris Convention allows inventors to file in one country and preserve their original filing date as they make arrangements to file patent applications in other signatory countries [18] within 12 months.

The common practice is to first file an application in the inventor's home nation, mostly for logistical convenience, and thereafter to file in other nations within 12 months after the application is translated. The Paris Convention allows filings in all countries to benefit the same original priority date in home country.

It is worth noting that in order to enjoy the benefit of 12 months period, multiple nation patents must be describing the same invention by the same inventor(s). Also, all intended filings in other countries have to be filed 12 months within the first country's filing date, i.e. the earliest priority date. There is no chain effect that allows you to claim the priority of a foreign filing, which claims the priority of another foreign filing and so on to extend back to beyond 12 months.

As illustrated in a hypothetical example in Fig. 3.5, Smith patent's Japanese filing does enjoy the benefit of its German filing date whereas its U.S. filing does not. The fact that the U.S. filing date is within one year from its Japanese filing date does not simply allow US application to benefit any foreign filing date because it has past beyond 1 year from its earliest German filing date.

---

[18] In practice, any application originating in a WPO member country will be accorded priority.

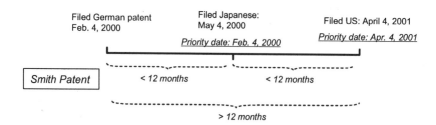

Fig. 3.5 Priority date and international filing.

3.13.2 *Patent Cooperation Treaty*

Another important international agreement regarding patent is the Patent Cooperation Treaty (PCT). PCT was formed at Washington D.C. in 1970 and has been amended and modified several times until 2001. PCT is a significant improvement over Paris Convention but not a replacement of Paris Convention. The PCT will not diminish any rights under Paris Convention. It is open to all state parties of Paris Convention and is administered by the WIPO.

The PCT provides a vehicle to allow an inventor seeking protection in multiple nations to file one-for-all instead of filing patents in each individual country. The inventor can file a patent in one country as if he is filing in all other countries of his desire. PCT is rather complicated, but the remaining of this section is set out to give you some basis of the Treaty.

International Filing and Priority Date

Under PCT an inventor can file an international patent at the Receiving Office of his home country, such as the USPTO, for U.S. and designate other PCT countries. Like filing a domestic application, you can also claim the priority of an early application occurred within 12 months under Paris Convention.

National Stage

National stage can be treated as if the patent application is filed domestically in each designated country. An international patent application can enter national stage no later than 30 months from the earliest effective filing date assuming it meets all the requirements of domestic application. Once an international patent application enters national stage, it will be treated the same as national application or domestic application. There are many advantages of using PCT to enter national stage as opposed to filing in each individual country because there is no duplicate document submission. The document submitted to the home Receiving Office will be automatically forwarded to each designated country.

Preliminary Search and Preliminary Examination

During the period from when an international patent application is filed to when it enters national stage, preliminary search by the International Search Authority (ISA) is always conducted and preliminary non-bonding written opinions are provided. Usually the international search report and written opinion are provided by the ISA nine months from the filing date. The search report and written opinion will list any publications and prior arts that the ISA finds relevant to the patent application and opinions on patentability of each claim. Optionally preliminary examination can also be requested.

The USPTO acts as an ISA for international applications filed in the U.S. Receiving Office of the USPTO to establish documentary search reports and provide written opinions. The European Patent Office (EPO) acts in similar capacity of ISA for European applications with certain limitations in the fields of biotechnology and business methods. The written opinions will be made available to the Offices of all designated countries and is available to the public for inspection after 30 months from the priority date.

The written opinion will be forwarded to the inventor as well. The inventor may choose to or not choose to reply to the written opinion. Also note that the written opinion is not an Office Action for any national stage application. It may provide a reference to be considered by the examiner during the national stage patent prosecution.

The PCT is a powerful vehicle for filing multinational patents. When properly used, the PCT can give you significant time while you are preparing for translation into designated country's language before the national stage is entered. The maximum delay from when the first patent application was filed until the national stage is entered is 30 months, in comparison to 12 months purely under Paris Convention.

PART 2 Fundamentals in Patenting

Chapter 4

How to Read a Patent

For various reasons, all inventors need to read patents. Unfortunately, the strange patent language makes this task a big undertaking for many of people. Also, a large percentage of U.S. patents are first filed in an inventor's home country and then translated into English to file in the U.S. How well a foreign patent has been translated greatly affects the readability of the patent as well.

Just like any sports or hobbies, the reading of patents improves with practice. The more you read, the better you get; there is no easy way around it. This chapter aims to give readers some tips on patent reading and hopefully helps them find the right starting point.

4.1   Anatomy of a Patent

4.1.1   *Patent Cover Page*

This section is intended to give you a complete reference of various parts of a patent. It is also recommended that you frequently come back to this section upon your actual reading of patents.

Each patent has a cover page that contains important information about the patent — often called bibliographical data. Figure 4.1 is an example of the cover page of a U.S. patent, for which a brief explanation of each main field is provided as below.

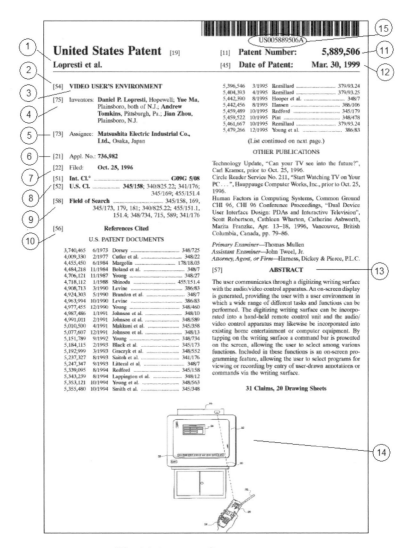

Fig. 4.1 Anatomy of patent cover page.

1. The last name of the first inventor.[1]

---

[1] Other than the showing of the name of the first inventor on the cover page, there is no difference between the first and subsequent inventors in terms of legal rights or any other aspects.

2. The number inside the bracket is called INID Code[2] and is defined by international agreement to indicate a specific field in bibliographic data of a patent. It is an acronym for "Internationally agreed Numbers for the Identification of (bibliographic) Data" and is widely used on the first page of patent documents in the same manner among all countries. Whether it is a U.S. patent, a Japanese or a European patent, all the fields on the cover page of the patent are labeled by the same code. The main benefits of INID code include improved access to information relating to patents and easy identification of various bibliographic data appearing on the first page of a patent document without knowledge of the language used.

3. The title of a patent — a name selected by the patentee to describe the invention.

4. The names of inventors and their residence.

5. The name of assignee (owner) of the patent.

6. Application number or series number, which is the number firstly assigned to the application when it was filed. This number is used as a reference during the entire patent prosecution period. Once a patent is issued, this number becomes less important.

7. Filing date. It is often related to the priority date of the patent.

8. U.S. and International classification (IPC). The classifications that are related to the field of the invention, which are labeled by the Patent Office. The U.S. and international classifications are different and they can be found at the USPTO website and WIPO website, respectively. An introduction of the U.S. classification and IPC structures is also given in Chapter 15. The classification information is useful when searching for relevant prior arts.

9. Field of search — the US classifications used in examiner's search strategy (for prior art) at the time of examination.

10. Reference cited. This is the reference cited by the inventor and is also called backward citation. See also Sections 3.11 and 8.3 for IDS.

11. Patent number — a number assigned by the USPTO to each issued patent chronologically. Currently it is in the 7 million range.

---

[2] Related document can be found at http://www.wipo.int/standards/en/pdf/03-09-01.pdf. It is also referred to as WIPO Standard ST.9.

12. Date of patent — the patent issue date. This is also the date when a patent becomes in force.

13. Abstract — a short description of the invention as is similar to the abstract of any technical paper. It is often an easy entry point for a reader to grasp the inventive concept in the patent.

14. An exemplary drawing of the patent. It is selected by the inventor or the examiner and intended to be representative of the invention.

15. Patent number with kind code. Every time a patent is published it is appended a kind code after the patent number to indicate type of publication. For example, for this US patent in the example, "A" indicates U.S. patent[3]. The patent kind code is explained in more detail in Appendix B.

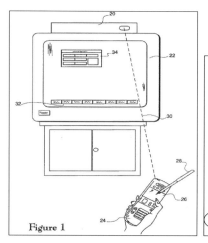

Fig. 4.2 Example of patent drawing and its reference in specification.

4.1.2   *Patent Drawings*

Figure 4.2 further illustrates exemplary drawings in a patent. When describing any component in a drawing, both figure number and component label in the figure are properly referenced in the specification.

---

[3] This is the old kind code, which is replaced by the new definition in January 2, 2001.

4.1.3 Patent Specification

Patent specification is the heart of the invention. Although it is the claim that constitutes final legal rights, without a solid support in the specification, the claim cannot stand by itself. Figure 4.3 shows an exemplary patent specification. Some key parts of the specification are explained below.

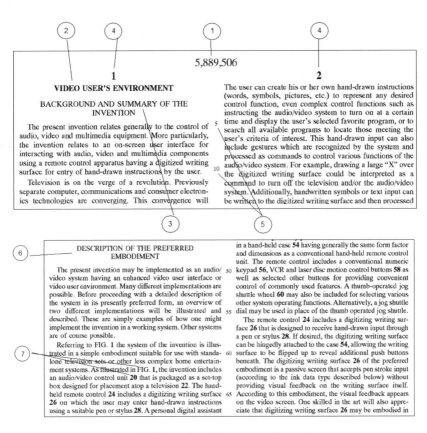

Fig. 4.3 Illustration of patent specification.

1. Patent number. Every page of the patent has a patent number shown on the top.
2. The title of invention.

3. Background/summary of the invention. This is often similar to the introduction in any technical paper, in which it describes the motivation of the invention (although not legally required) and summary of the invention to give user a snapshot of what the invention is about.

4. Column number. In every page of the spec all text is labeled by its column and line number. This is particularly useful when the patent examiner cites a prior art to reject your application. You may use the column/line number to quickly locate the text being cited.

5. Line number – used in combination of column number to locate any text in the specification.

6. Description of the preferred embodiment – the main part of specification.

7. Figure and component label – used to reference a component in the figure.

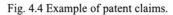

FIG. 21 gives another example of the edit distance computation technique. As before, strings of alphabetic characters are compared for demonstration purposes. As previously noted, this is done for convenience, to simplify the illustration, and should not be interpreted as implying that the strings must be first converted to alphanumeric text before the comparisons are made. Rather, the procedure illustrated in FIGS. 20 and 21 are performed on the respective stroke data (vector quantized symbols) of the respective stored annotation and input query strings.

FIG. 21 specifically illustrates the technique that may be used to perform an approximate match (word spotting). In FIG. 21 the stored annotation "This is compression," is compared with the query string "compass." Note how the matched region 430 is extracted from the full string of the stored annotation by scanning the last row of the table to find the indices that represent the lowest value. Note that the first (initializing) row in FIG. 21 is all 0s—this allows the approximate matching procedure to start anywhere along the database string.

The presently preferred edit distance procedure is enhanced over the conventional procedures described in the literature. In addition to the three basic editing operations (delete a character, insert a character, and substitute one character for another), it is useful to add two new operations when comparing pen stroke sequences. These new operations are "split" (substitute two strokes for one stroke) and "merge" (substitute one stroke for two strokes). These additional operations allow for errors made in stroke segmentation and generally leads to more accurate results.

The use of our enhanced edit distance procedure is illustrated in FIG. 21. In FIG. 21 the split operation is used to substitute the letters "re" in "compress" for the letter "a" in "compass." Note that the backtracking arrow in FIG. 21 spans one row but two columns, thereby signifying the multicharacter (merge) substitution. Hence the edit distance

The foregoing discussion discloses and describes exemplary embodiments of the present invention. One skilled in the art will readily recognize from such discussion and from the accompany drawings and claims, that various changes, modifications and variations can be made therein without departing from the spirit and scope of the invention as defined in the following claims.

What is claimed is:

1. An audio/video system having an enhanced video user environment, comprising:

an audio/video control apparatus for selectively performing predetermined audio/video control functions in accordance with a user's selection, said control apparatus including a port for coupling to a video display apparatus for displaying video material;

a remote control apparatus having a digitizing writing surface for entry of hand-drawn instructions by a user, said remote control apparatus communicating with said audio/video control apparatus;

a processor communicating with at least one of said audio/video control apparatus and said remote control apparatus for controlling operation of said video display apparatus in accordance with said hand-drawn instructions wherein said processor has an associated database of stored annotations and wherein said processor compares said stored annotations with said hand-drawn instructions by peforming an edit distance analysis to account for mismatch between said stored annotations and said hand-drawn instructions.

2. The system of claim 1 wherein said remote control comprises a hand-held push-button remote control structure with said digitizing writing surface incorporated into said structure.

3. The system of claim 1 wherein said remote control communicates with said audio/video control apparatus by infrared signals.

Fig. 4.4 Example of patent claims.

4.1.4 *Patent Claims*

Patent claim is the most important part of the patent because it describes your legal rights. It is always appended to the end of the specification and starts with languages such as "What is claimed:", "I claim:" or "We claim:" etc. Figure 4.4 shows an example of claim for the same patent we have shown earlier. The key parts labeled are:

1. The start of the claim.
2. Independent claim.
3. Dependent claim as it references "claim 1" in the text – it means it depends on independent claim 1.

The claim structure and how to construe a claim will be further explained later in this chapter.

4.2 Find Your Easiest Entry Point — A First Glance

For people who are new to patents, the challenge in reading a patent is to quickly grasp the essence of the invention without being overwhelmed by so many legal terms that may otherwise confuse the reader. Similar to reading any technical article, your entry point starts with the title of the patent, abstract and summary of the invention.

When a patent is well written, except its claims, it should read as natural as any technical paper. The rule is simple: if you can understand a concept from the short version, you should not need reading the long text version. Therefore, you should always try to understand a patent from reading into its title and abstract first, then the background of the invention, then the summary of the invention. Finally, read into details in the patent specification when needed. Also, you may want to refer to some drawings to help with your understanding of the patent.

There are times when people use exactly the same language in the summary of the invention as in the claims in order to avoid any potential legal issues (see Section 7.1). By doing so, the summary of the invention becomes extremely difficult to comprehend. If you encounter such summary of the invention, your best bet is to read further into the detailed description of the invention to get a better understanding.

4.3   Understand Embodiments of a Patent

In accordance with the present invention, a screen oriented display processing system is provided for the freeform entry of informational data including a display means, a.data entry means for entering informational data on said display means, a gesture entering means for entering freeform gestural data on said display, said gestural data representing a gesture associated with at least a portion of said informational data on said display, an assignment means responsive to the entry of said gesture for assigning an operation representative of said gesture to said portion of said informational data, and an implementing means responsive to said assignment means for implementing said operation on said portion of said informational data. The assignment means includes means for establishing a determination of structure of said informational data sufficient to accomplish said operation.

In accordance with another aspect of the present invention, a graphic editing system is provided including a data interface surface and user controllable means for generating information on said surface. The system comprises first means responsive to a user action that generates a line image on the surface for performing an operation on at least a portion of said information, said line image having a set of instructions associated therewith, second means responsive to said set of instructions for selectively analyzing, organizing, and rearranging information displayed on said surface, and third means for implementing said operation on said information according to said instructions.

In accordance with another aspect of the invention, a graphic editing system is provided including a data .interface surface and user controllable means for generating information on said surface. The system comprises first means responsive to a user action that generates a line image on said surface for selecting at least a portion of said information, said first line having a set of instructions associated therewith, second means responsive to said set of instructions for selectively analyzing, organizing and rear-

Fig. 4.5 Three embodiments of an invention.

A patent may include several different yet related inventive concepts, or any variations of the key idea. These variations are often described in multiple embodiments of the patent. The purpose of disclosing multiple embodiments is to lay a ground support on the scope of the invention. Any variations or extension from the key concept entitles the patent owner to claim additional space by making the invention broad.

The places to identify embodiments of a patent are usually Summary of the Invention or in Detailed Description of the Invention. Figure 4.5 shows an example of the summary of the invention, in which three embodiments are disclosed to describe three slightly different systems.

4.4 Understand Claims

Claim, to many inventors, is the most difficult part of a patent to comprehend. However, it is the most important part of an invention as well. It spells out clearly the legal rights the patent owner is entitled to. Understanding the claims of a patent is the key to determining if a given product or process infringes the patent. This section attempts to give readers a quick introduction on how to read claims.[4]

4.4.1 *Patent Claim Basics*

There are several basics about claims:

1. Each claim is a sentence. It starts with a capital letter and ends with a period.
2. Claims always start with number 1.
3. A patent can have many or few claims. A claim can be long or short. There are no rules how many claims you can have, and how long each claim must be. There is at least one claim in a patent, however.
4. There are two types of claims: independent and dependent. As the name imply, independent claims can be interpreted stand-alone

---

[4] Design patents and plant patents have similar claims, which is a single claim referring to the drawings or description. In science and technology, we are mostly dealing with utility patents. Therefore, our discussion focuses only on utility patents.

without associating with any other claims. A patent must have at least one independent claim.

5. A dependent claim, on the other hand, should only be interpreted in the context of the independent claim it refers to and inherits all the limitations in that independent claim. A dependent claim, for example, may appear like "The system of claim 1, further comprising ...."

6. A dependent claim can refer to another dependent claim, which refers to another dependent claim in a chain, and traces back all the way to its root independent claim. In the same token, the dependent claim at the end includes all the limitations in all the other dependent claims it refers to in the chain, and the root independent claim.

<u>Why Dependent Claims?</u>

As can be seen, a dependent claim can only have more limitations than its preceding independent claim. Therefore, a dependent claim is narrower in its scope than the independent claim it refers to. Then one may ask: why do we still need dependent claims if it is not going to make the claims any broader?

Let us look at this scenario: suppose you claim someone stole your poncho and show them that it slips right over your head and fits you, your evidence may not be convincing because the poncho is pretty much one-size-fits-all. However, if you claim someone stole your shirt and show that the shirt fits you perfectly at collar and sleeves, it would be more convincing because the same shirt cannot easily fit into everyone the perfect way as it does on you.

In analogy, if you sue someone for infringing your patent, you would like the accused product to fit to your claims as tight as possible. You would like the accused product to infringe not only your independent claims, but also dependent claims. The more claims they infringe, the stronger case you will have.

Limitations of Dependent Claims

Because dependent claims include all limitations in its preceding independent claim, in order for a product to infringe your dependent claim, it must infringe your independent claim. If a product does not infringe your independent claim, it is not infringing your dependent claims either.

4.4.2 *Patent Claim Structure*

A great deal associated with the reading of claims is to interpret the claims according to their structures and limitations therefore to understand the scope of the exclusive rights patent owner is entitled to. This process is also referred to as "construing" claims. Knowing the claim structure is rather important in construing any claims.

An independent claim usually includes three parts: preamble, transitional phrase and main body, as shown in Fig. 4.6.

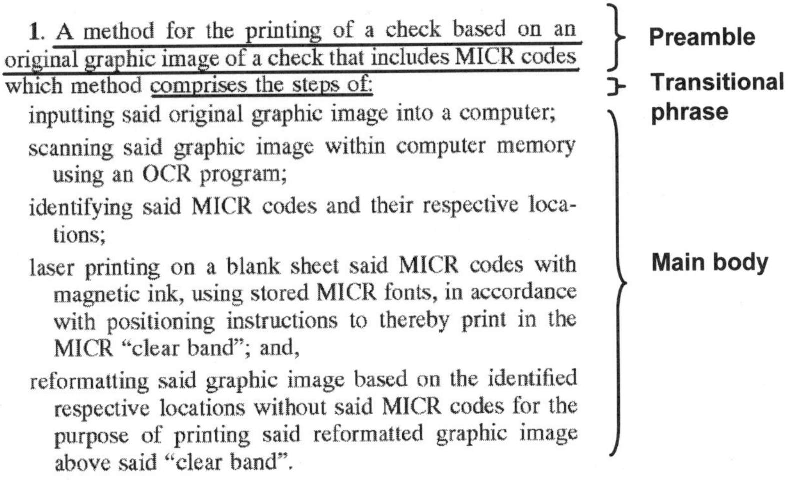

1. A method for the printing of a check based on an original graphic image of a check that includes MICR codes — **Preamble**

which method comprises the steps of: — **Transitional phrase**

    inputting said original graphic image into a computer;

    scanning said graphic image within computer memory using an OCR program;

    identifying said MICR codes and their respective locations;

    laser printing on a blank sheet said MICR codes with magnetic ink, using stored MICR fonts, in accordance with positioning instructions to thereby print in the MICR "clear band"; and, — **Main body**

    reformatting said graphic image based on the identified respective locations without said MICR codes for the purpose of printing said reformatted graphic image above said "clear band".

Fig. 4.6 Three basic components of a claim.

Preamble

The preamble is to set forth the general technical environment of the invention. For example, a claim to a method for printing a check out of an MICR code might have the preamble as shown in Fig. 4.6. The preamble is usually not considered to be a legally limiting constraint on the invention. However, some people attempt to avoid the claim being any narrow and simply write the preamble as "A method" or "A system".

Transitional Phrase

Transitional phrase usually comes as "comprises of", "consists of", or "consists essentially of". Their meanings are as below.

1. "Comprises of" is an open term. It is a short way of saying "including but not limited to the following items". Therefore, "comprising of A+B" in the claim will cover the case of "A+B+C". The fewer items in the "comprising of" combination, the broader the claim is. In practice, an inventor determines the minimum number of elements needed for the invention and only include those minimum required elements in a "comprising of" open combination to make the claim as broad as possible. Any optional element should generally not be included in the "comprising of" claim.

2. "Consisting of" is a closed term. It is a short way of saying "including and only including the following items". The "consisting of" term is usually used in chemical composition invention. A "consisting of A+B" in the claim will NOT cover the case of "A+B+C".

3. "Consisting essentially of" is a short way of saying "mainly including the following items". The "consisting essentially of A+B" would cover "A+B+C" if C is not affecting the basic characteristics of the invention. Again, the "consisting essentially of" is usually used in chemical composition invention.

Transitional phrase is rather important as it directly affects the scope of the claims. As illustrated above, all three elements A, B and C are included in the main body of the claim (as will be explained next) using different transitional phrases. The result gives you different legal rights.

In another so-called Jepson type claim, often marked by a phrase such as "wherein the improvement comprises" in its transitional phrase, the preamble recites all the elements deemed to be of known art, and the body of the claim (as will be explained next) includes only new elements that constitute improvements over existing art. Jepson claim does seem to pose some limitations when it comes to construe claims. In the Jepson format, the preambles have been held to constitute limitations in the past; whereas it has not been the case for the claims presented in other formats.

Jepson type claim has been favored by the USPTO[5] to use for the improvement inventions; however, it is not strictly enforced. When you are in doubt as to whether a claim is indeed a Jepson claim, and how to interpret the scope of claims, always consult a patent attorney or agent for advice.

Main Body of Claims

The main body follows the preamble and transitional phrase and lists the main components of the invention in a legal form. The following rules may help you identify these elements and properly construe claims.

1. "Said" or "the" is often used to refer to a previously defined element. When an element is firstly defined or introduced in the claim, it should precede with "a". For example, in the above example in Fig. 4.6, the "said MICR codes" refers to the MICR codes mentioned in the preamble, which is the MICR code included in a check. In the same claim, in the last element "on the identified respective locations" refers to the location identified by the previous step "identifying said MICR codes and their respective location". It is important to note that when you see "said" or "the" preceding an element, such element must have already been defined early in the claim and it is not a new item.

---

[5] 37 CFR 1.75(e).

2. Unless explicitly described, the order of elements is not important. Take the claim in Fig. 4.6, for example, there are five steps as labeled in Table 4.1. As commented in the "Remark" column, Steps 1, 2, 3 are required to perform in the order they appear. However, Steps 4 and 5 only need to happen after Step 3, but the order between Steps 4 and 5 is not important. In the same token, a system implementing Steps "1, 2, 3, 4, 5" or Steps "1, 2, 3, 5, 4" both will infringe the claim.

Table 4.1 The order of elements in a patent claim.

Steps	Claim Elements	Remark
1	inputting said original graphic image into a computer;	
2	scanning said graphic image within computer memory using an OCR program;	Depends on "said graphic image" in Step 1.
3	identifying said MICR codes and their respective locations;	Implicitly requires "scanned image" in Step 2.
4	laser printing on a blank sheet said MICR codes with magnetic ink, using stored MICR fonts, in accordance with positioning instructions to thereby print in the MICR "clear band"; and	Use identified MICR image in Step 3.
5	reformatting said graphic image based on the identified respective locations without said MICR codes for the purpose of printing said reformatted graphic image above said "clear band".	Use identified location in Step 3.

In the remainder of this chapter, we will work on numerous real examples of claims.

4.5   Different Types of Claims

From a reader's perspective, there are several different claim types that are worth mentioning. Although they appear to be different, they are often of the same claim structure and you should be comfortable interpreting those claims.

4.5.1 *Product, System, Composition and Apparatus Claim*

Example 1: A Product or System

"A flying spot raster output scanning optical <u>system</u> for adjusting the resolution of a scan beam along the scan line <u>comprising</u>:

a laser diode source which emits a coherent light beam, collimating means for collimating said emitted light beam,

first optical means for converging the cross-scan portion of said collimated beam,

a rotatable aperture for selectively blocking said light beam from said first optical beam, means for rotating said rotatable aperture,

a rotating polygon mirror with a plurality of facets for reflecting said beam from said rotatable aperture second optical means for converging the scan and cross-scan portions of the reflected beam to form a scan beam along said scan line,

whereby said rotatable aperture adjusts the resolution of said scan beam along said scan line."[6]

Example 2: A Product or System

"A scanning <u>system</u> <u>comprising</u>:

a first laser source, emitting a first beam in a first direction;

a second laser source, emitting a second beam in a second direction;

and a roof mirror configured to direct the first beam and the second beam so that the first beam and second beam have a substantially coincident virtual source point."[7]

---

[6] US 5517215
[7] US 5519432

Example 3: Apparatus

"An <u>apparatus</u> for printing on a substrate, <u>comprising</u>:

means for determining a first set of heating elements corresponding to a position where a colorant is intended to be applied to a substrate;

means for determining a second set of heating elements which are immediately adjacent to said first set of heating elements;

means for energizing said first set and said second set of heating elements to deposit an image-enhancing coating on said substrate;

and means for energizing said first set of heating elements to deposit a colorant on the image-enhancing coating without energizing said second set of heating elements."[8]

Example 4: Composition

"An ink composition consisting essentially of

(1) a quaternary compound selected from the group consisting of
   (a) imidazolinium quaternary salts,
   (b) phosphonium quaternary salts, and
   (c) ammonium quaternary salts;
(2) a liquid ink vehicle;
(3) a paper-curl reducing compound;
(4) a lightfastness component;
(5) a lightfastness antioxidant;
(6) a substantially water soluble organic salt or a substantially water soluble inorganic salt;
(7) a biocide; and
(8) a colorant."[9]

---

[8] US 5512930
[9] US 6086661

The commonality of these various uses of the product/apparatus claim is that they all follow the same claim structure previously discussed. In order to infringe the claim, one needs to practice all elements in the claim.

4.5.2 *Product-by-Process Claim*

Product-by-process claim is used to claim a product by describing the process or method of its manufacture. It is not commonly used, but it is an alternative approach to the traditional system or apparatus claim, which may not be feasible to describe the structural differences between the invention and similar products made by other processes. The following is an example of product-by-process claim:

Example 5: Product-by-process Claim

"A process for the preparation of a fuser member consisting of applying to a fuser supporting substrate a coating mixture of a fluoropolymer, and an aliphatic alcohol, and wherein the fluoropolymer is a terpolymer of vinylidene fluoride, hexafluoropropylene and tetrafluoroethylene, magnesium hydroxide, calcium hydroxide, and bisphenol curative in methanol with a viscosity of less than about 1,000 to about 2,000 centipoise after about 24 hours"[10]

Product-by-process claim poses limitations on the process being used in the manufacture of an article. If we construe the product-by-process claim as we do on other types of claims, a similar product made by a process different from the process specified in the product-by-process claim is not infringing. There have been divided opinions, however, on Federal Circuits on whether a product-by-process claim of similar product made by a different process is patentable. Dave Fox's article gives a good summary on this issue[11].

---

[10] Claim 16 of US Patent 5,501,881.

[11] Dave L. Fox, "Product-By-Process Claims: A Possible Answer Under Phillips to the Atlantic – Scripps Schism", Intellectual Property Today, Oct. 2006, pp. 33–37.

4.5.3   *Method Claim*

Method claim has the same claim structure as product, system and apparatus claim. It can be recognized easily by the term "method" in its preamble, and it is often used to describe a series of steps in achieving a function. The following is an example of method claim.

Example 6: Method Claim

"A <u>method</u> of sending data from a data sender to a data receiver through a data sending medium, <u>comprising</u>:

continuously sending data transmission commands from said data receiver to said data sender prior to the transfer of the data from said data sender to said data receiver;

detecting the data transmission commands including a transmission error or identical data transmission commands at the data sender to thereby control the reception of the data transmission commands;

starting the transmission of the data from said data sender to said data receiver based on said continuously-transmitted data transmission commands;

monitoring a form of the transmission of the data from said data sender to said data receiver;

and terminating the transmission of said data transmission commands, based on the result of said monitoring;

wherein the step of detecting includes abandoning a first received data transmission command including the transmission error or the data transmission command when a second received data transmission command is identical to the first received data transmission command."[12]

---

[12] US 5896413

4.5.4 *Means-plus-function Claim*

The apparatus claim in Example 3 is actually a means-plus-function claim, but worth mentioning because of the special way claims are construed.

As stated in the U.S. Patent Law[13]: "An element in a claim for a combination may be expressed as a means or step for performing a specified function without the recital of structure, material, or acts in support thereof, and such claim shall be construed to cover the corresponding structure, material, or acts described in the specification and equivalents thereof."

In Example 3, each step in the claim needs to be construed in the same structure or material as disclosed in the specification. This practice has greatly reduced the scope of means-plus-function claim that may appear to be broad.

4.5.5 *Software or Business Method Claim*

There is no such software, hardware or business method type claim, but several types of claims mentioned above can well suit the purpose of describing a software, hardware or business method. Let us visit the U.S. patent No. 5,960,411 ('411) Amazon.com patent. The patent relates to a method for ordering items over the Internet through a user single-action (e.g. one click of a mouse button) through which the ordered merchandise and user ID are transmitted to the server and the server looks up pre-stored user information to complete the order without asking user for more action.

The invention is a combination of business method (for conducting eCommerce) and software system (associated web platform for ordering). Table 4.2 shows four independent claims: Claims 1, 6, 9 and 11. Among these claims, Claims 1 and 11 are method claims; Claims 6 and 9 are system claims. As illustrated, to claim a software or business method, variations of a product/apparatus/system and method claims can be used in combination to cover various aspects of the invention. In light of this

---

[13] 35 USC 112 sixth paragraph.

Table 4.2 Diversity of independent claims.

1.A <u>method</u> of placing an order for an item comprising:
under control of a client system,
  displaying information identifying the item; and
  in response to only a single action being performed, sending a request to order the item
    along with an identifier of a purchaser of the item to a server system;
under control of a single-action ordering component of the server system,
  receiving the request;
  retrieving additional information previously stored for the purchaser identified by the
    identifier in the received request; and
generating an order to purchase the requested item for the purchaser identified by the
  identifier in the received request using the retrieved additional information; and
fulfilling the generated order to complete purchase of the item whereby the item is ordered
  without using a shopping cart ordering model.

6.A client <u>system</u> for ordering an item comprising:
an identifier that identifies a customer;
a display component for displaying information identifying the item;
a single-action ordering component that in response to performance of only a single action,
  sends a request to a server system to order the identified item, the request including the
  identifier so that the server system can locate additional information needed to complete
  the order and so that the server system can fulfill the generated order to complete
  purchase of the item; and
a shopping cart ordering component that in response to performance of an add-to-
  shopping-cart action, sends a request to the server system to add the item to a shopping
  cart.

9.A server <u>system</u> for generating an order comprising:
a shopping cart ordering component; and
a single-action ordering component including:
  a data storage medium storing information for a plurality of users;
  a receiving component for receiving requests to order an item,
  a request including an indication of one of the plurality of users, the request being sent in
response to only a single action being performed; and
an order placement component that retrieves from the data storage medium information
  for the indicated user and that uses the retrieved information to place an order for the
  indicated user for the item; and
an order fulfillment component that completes a purchase of the item in accordance with
  the order placed by the single-action ordering component.

11.A <u>method</u> for ordering an item using a client system, the method comprising:
displaying information identifying the item and displaying an indication of a single action
  that is to be performed to order the identified item; and
in response to only the indicated single action being performed, sending to a server system
  a request to order the identified item
whereby the item is ordered independently of a shopping cart model and the order is
  fulfilled to complete a purchase of the item.

example, how to diversify claims to obtain a broader protection will be further discussed in Section 7.5.

4.6   Understand the Scope of the Invention

We have walked through claim structures and types. An important purpose the claims serve, more than any other parts of the specification, is the interpretation of the scope of the invention. It is reflective of the exclusive rights the patent owner is entitled to and is often a critical part of patent reading.

Basically, determining the scope of the invention is about construing a claim structure in the broadest way it can be to one ordinary skilled in the art without losing support from the specification. In practical, you would need to figure out the number of steps/components that comprise the claimed system and any limiting language in the independent claim. The following example, as shown in Fig. 4.7, compares the scope of three different parts of the specification: drawing, summary of the invention and the claim.

From both drawing and the summary of invention, the invention appears to be a remote control device with a writing surface and a stylus that uses hand-drawn instructions to control the TV or video systems. Hmm, pretty neat idea, and may be a useful product!

Let us take a look at the first independent claim. First, an "audio/video" appears in the preamble of the claim, and "video" further appears in the first element of the claim. Therefore, the scope of the remote control is further limited to a video environment.

Next, the transitional phrase "comprising" recites an open term, i.e. the elements possessed in an infringing product need to have at least those to be disclosed in the main body of the claim but should not be limited only to those elements.

Next, the second element of the claim contains "writing surface" and "hand-drawn instructions", which is consistent with the summary of the invention. The invented device must have a writing surface and a stylus to enter hand-drawn instructions.

Next, the third element contains a processor for matching hand-drawn instructions and pre-stored annotations. It has to be able to store a series of hand-drawn commands and be able to "recognize" hand-drawn instructions by matching with stored hand-drawn commands. With such limitation, the invention does not cover the scenario where user uses the writing tablet to just tap and select control keys.

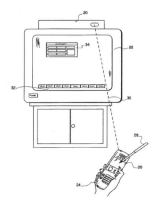

The present invention takes a fresh approach to the problem. Although the hand-held remote with push buttons may still be used, the present invention provides a digitizing writing surface through which the user may enter hand-drawn instructions. These instructions can be handwritten text, symbols or even pictures, all of which are written to the digitized writing surface using a pen or stylus. Such a means for controlling the system and providing input appeals to a broader range of users than does a conventional keyboard. Through the mechanism of providing hand-drawn instructions, complex systems can be controlled with ease.

1. An audio/video system having an enhanced video user environment, comprising:
an audio/video control apparatus for selectively performing predetermined audio/video control functions in accordance with a user's selection, said control apparatus including a port for coupling to a video display apparatus for displaying video material;
a remote control apparatus having a digitizing writing surface for entry of hand-drawn instructions by a user, said remote control apparatus communicating with said audio/video control apparatus;
a processor communicating with at least one of said audio/video control apparatus and said remote control apparatus for controlling operation of said video display apparatus in accordance with said hand-drawn instructions wherein said processor has an associated database of stored annotations and wherein said processor compares said stored annotations with said hand-drawn instructions by peforming an edit distance analysis to account for mismatch between said stored annotations and said hand-drawn instructions.

Fig. 4.7 Limitations in the claim.

Lastly, the "edit distance analysis" further limits the matching of hand-drawing instruction to the "edit distance" algorithm. What exactly is "edit distance"? You may refer to the specification for descriptions and examples. Clearly, this does not cover the use of image matching of hand-drawn instructions and stored commends as image matching is not edit-distance.

After reading all limitations of the claim, you probably realize that the claim is actually much narrower than what appears to be in the drawing or summary of the invention. Fatally, the "edit distance analysis" opens the door for many possible invent-around. If someone is doing everything the same as described in the claim, except using an image matching algorithm to recognize hand-drawn instructions, he is not infringing the patent claim.

The scope of the invention, as reflected in the claim, directly impacts the strength of the patent. If your claim is rather narrow, and there may be many ways to get around, your patent may not be as effective or enforceable.

4.7 What to Look For When You Read a Patent

Depending on your objective, you should be looking for different things when you are reading a patent.

4.7.1 *If You are Filing a Patent*

<u>Prior Art is Not Limited to Claims</u>

If you are conducting a preliminary patent search before filing a patent, and search for prior arts to make sure your invention is patentable, you can pretty much skip reading claims and concentrate on the specification. Anything described in the specification, regardless of whether being claimed or not, would be considered as prior art and no longer be patentable.

Through the reading of specification, just like literature research of an academic paper, ask yourself whether someone has done it before rather than what other people have claimed.

Look for Your Novelty and Nonobviousness Against Prior Art

If you see something related to your invention, or broader than your invention, do not let it discourage you. For example, you might find a prior art on a telephone system that mentioned nothing about the speaker phone you are inventing. As long as your improvement of adding a speaker phone to the traditional telephone is not being done before, your invention should be novel.

In addition, you should always ask yourself whether your invention would be an obvious improvement over prior arts. If your idea is close to the prior art, read into all multiple embodiments of the prior art as some variations exhibited in other embodiments may be overlooked yet can render your ideas obvious.

Determining obviousness is a gray area. But make a judgment call to yourself, and if you think it is not obvious, then go for it. Later in this book, we will discuss pitfalls and tips how to overcome rejections should patent examiner reject your claims on obviousness.

4.7.2   *If a Reference Patent is Cited For Rejecting Your Claims*

Very often in patent prosecution, the examiner may reject your claims based on one or more reference prior arts. The examiner cites a prior art reference in the Office Action and gives detailed statement how each of the element of your claim is recited in the reference. For each element of your claim, the examiner lists in what reference prior art and where in the prior art your claim element has been covered.

When this happens, you will need to read into the cited prior art, most likely a patent. Similar to the discussion in the last section, your focus is on the specification of the patent, particularly text that has been cited by the examiner.

In Chapter 9, we are going to cover entirely what you can do to overcome rejections. At the moment, you should be comfortable reading other people's patent should your claims be rejected with reference to a prior art.

4.7.3   *If You are Making a Product*

When a manufacturer is ready to launch a product, they often hire a professional law firm to conduct so-called product clearance. The objective is to search for prior arts to determine whether they run the risk of infringing other people's patents.

<u>Infringement Can Only Happen to Claims</u>

The task of reading a patent in light of a product basically becomes the patent infringement detection, for which the center of attention is claims. You will never infringe someone's specification. You can only infringe someone's claims.

Your effort should be focused on comparing your product features and their claims and determine whether your product has every single element/feature as described in their independent claim. If you read a patent's abstract and summary of the invention and find it broad enough to cover all your product features, do not let it discourage you. They may have a broad spec but a narrow claim. If you see something in the specification but not appearing in the claim, that should not worry you[14].

One aspect you should look into is how broad other people's claims can be. This has to do with how to construe the claims based on what has been disclosed in the specification. Although the claim structures do allow people to claim broadly than possibly disclosed in the specification, at this stage, you should not construe other people's claims too broadly that it may pre-maturely kill your product idea.

Another thing to watch for is the means-plus-function claim, as explained earlier in this chapter. If a means-plus-function claim appears to cover your product, you need to check the structure of features in their specification and determine whether your product rides exactly on the

---

[14] There may be chances that this information is patented elsewhere. And that may be the reason the inventor of the current patent cannot claim such in his own patent.

same feature as in the claims and on the same structure in their specification. You do not need to be a legal expert, but you need to be aware of the means-plus-function claims that are very often narrower than what they appear to be.

What is Your Choice If You May be Infringing Other People's Claims

Last, if you do determine that your product has a high probability of infringing other people's claims, you can either decide to license to such patent, or invent around by changing your product features to get around their claims. Attorney's rule: Do not put in writing in any email or report saying that you may be or are infringing someone's patent. Discuss this matter face to face or on the phone.

4.7.4   *If You are Catching an Infringer*

Unlike previous scenarios, now you have a patent in hand and you are trying to determine if any identified product is infringing your patent. The approach is similar to infringement detection as discussed in the last section, but your task may be more difficult because you only have limited information about the identified product regarding how it works inside. Any further investigation about the identified product may require reverse engineering (RE) effort, which is done by people with special expertise and equipment.

Any reverse engineering effort can be costly. Before determining whether to pursue any reverse engineering work on any infringement case, your initial assessment will be very critical. You may want to keep the following in mind when investigating any product for possible infringement:

1. Concentrate on your independent claims and examine the identified product to see whether it has all the features in the claim. If the product does not fit into your claim, do not let it discourage you. Try to "stretch" your claim and construe to the broadest extent as possible and see if your claim can fit into the product.

2. If you are missing evidence but you have a reasonable belief that the identified product may be doing the way described in the claim, recommend RE work to further conduct investigation.

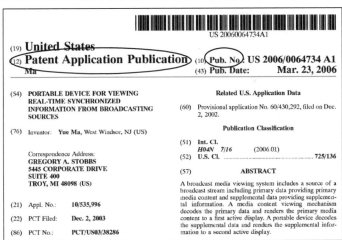

Fig. 4.8 Cover page of issued patent and patent publication.

Your technical assessment is not any legal opinion. You can be aggressive in identifying and suspecting any infringement case and bringing it to the attention of your legal counsel. Patent infringement analysis may require the assistance of both reverse engineering and legal professionals. However, your initial technical assessment is the most important step in detecting and proving of any patent infringement.

4.8   Published Patent Application

As mentioned in previous chapters, a patent application will be automatically published at USPTO website 18 months from its filing date. The cover page of a published patent application is similar to that of a granted patent, as illustrated in Fig. 4.8.

The key difference appears in the text "United States Patent Application Publication" instead of "United States Patent". Also, the publication is labeled as "Pub. No." vs. "Patent No." in granted patent. In addition to the difference of cover pages for granted patent and published patent application, there are several things you need to know.

1. Patent applications have claims but do not have any legal rights. Any patent application has to undergo the lengthy examination by the USPTO, and eventually the patent claims may not be granted at all, or only a subset of claims may be granted. Therefore, a patent application is not enforceable until it is granted.
2. A published patent application can be considered prior art although they are not granted. Since they are published, just like any publications (academic journal, conference), they are considered known to the public.

When it comes to reading a published patent application, you can skip the claims and only concentrate on the specification and understanding of the essence of the invention. You may be reading a patent application for patenting purpose; or for examining a cited prior art in association with an Office rejection. However, you do not need to read a patent application for infringement detection purpose because the application is not enforceable.

Chapter 5

Innovation Harvesting

You may have many ideas or very few ideas, big ideas or trivial ideas. Obviously, it is not economical to patent every single idea. The key is to identify the inventive concept that should be patented, requiring some basic knowledge about patent laws regarding patentability, as outlined in Section 3.5. The conversion of ideas to patents is a business decision resulting from the balancing of anticipated strength of the invention, market potential and budget constraint. This chapter walks you through various processes of the inventing stage — a stage that is the most crucial to the success of your innovation.

5.1   Knowing the Art

Inventing and filing patents do not require you to do any patent search. However, knowing the art is essential to your inventing process. You do not need to know every single patent there is before or during your invention, but it will be to your advantage to keep abreast of the latest advancement in your field of invention since your patent application will be examined against other patents and publications in the same field.

If you have been working in the same field for a number of years, you are probably already on top of the latest advancement. If you are new to the field, you are encouraged to do a little search so you are not re-inventing the wheel.

Patenting is about claiming your property that people have not claimed before. Therefore, knowing the art in the field of your invention is important in getting an intuition what has been claimed so you can be confident that your invention can stand on its own. The next section walks you through patentability test to help you distinguish your invention from existing known art in the field.

5.2   Patentability Test

The patentability test is the same test that any patent examiner would use in patent examination. Section 3.5 gives you a nutshell of patent laws related to patentability. This section is intended to give you an introduction on how the patentability test is being used in practice, and to give you a better understanding in this aspect through some case laws.

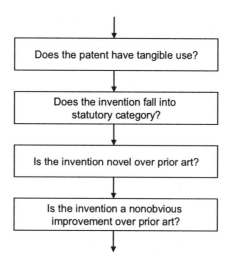

Fig. 5.1 Patentability test.

As introduced previously, laws related to patentability are subject matter and conditions of patentability. Particularly, the fundamentals of subject matter test are the usefulness of subject matter and statutory category of your claims. The fundamentals of conditions for patentability are novelty and nonobviousness. Given any new idea to be considered for patenting, you should run the following test, as illustrated in Fig. 5.1, to make sure at least you think it is patentable. The remaining of this section gives detailed explanation for each step.

5.2.1 *Subject Matter/Tangible Usefulness Test*

As mentioned previously, the key for any invention to be patentable is that it has to be useful. Abstract useful things and things formed by natural process are not patentable subject matter. To give you a better understanding, Table 5.1 shows some examples of patentable and unpatentable subject matters, primarily based on its tangible usefulness.

Table 5.1 Examples of patentability test.

Inventions	Patentability Test
DCT (Discrete Cosine Transform)	Unpatentable for its abstract, nontangible real use
A compression utilizing DCT to compress and decompress an image	Patentable software subject matter for its practical use. The software can be treated as a process for compressing or decompressing an image for efficient storage or media streaming.
Hidden Markov Model (HMM)	Unpatentable as an abstract formula.
A speech recognition algorithm using HMM	Patentable for its practical use. The software can be treated as a process.
A survey paper about the state-of-the-art technologies in early cancer diagnosis	Unpatentable for lack of real application. It is the actual technology being surveyed that bears practical use (for cancer diagnosis) not the survey paper. The survey does not belong to any of the process, machine, manufacture or composition of matters. This would be a very good academic paper though.
An experimental study of efficient compression algorithms	Unpatentable for lack of practical use. The study and experiments do not belong to any of process, machine, manufacture or composition of matters. The study would be a very useful academic paper.
A graphic widget for displaying weather information real-time on the computer screen	Patentable graphical user interface invention. The idea seems simple, yet it is patentable. The software can be considered as a process. The device (computer) having such widget on the display can be considered as a machine.
A system for uploading your own picture anywhere from your camera phone to a server and order a post card integrating your picture in it and be sent to anywhere in the world.	Patentable for its obvious tangible use. It is a business method and software patent.

I would like to particularly make a note of the last two examples of patentable subject matter. Scientists and engineers who are experts in highly complex techniques have often neglected graphical user interface or business method patents that seem to be trivial. These trivial inventions, once made into claims, can be quite powerful in excluding others because it is easy to detect if someone is infringing the patent.

5.2.2 *Statutory Categories and Case Study*

If you are at an early stage of your innovation and wonder whether it is really patentable, first test out whether they may fall into one of those statutory categories of invention, i.e. a machine, a process, manufacture or composition of matters. The following case study gives you an example how the subject matter patentability is being considered at the Federal Circuit. Some various aspects may be put into your own test.

Table 5.2 Statutory category in case study.

Allowed claims	Reasoning for allowance
The claims 1–10, with claim 1 independent, read as: A <u>method</u> of embedding supplemental data in a signal, comprising of: … list of steps …	directed to a process of encoding signal (one of the statutory categories); therefore are allowed by USPTO.
Claims 11-13 with independent claim read as: An <u>arrangement</u> for embedding supplemental data in a signal including: … encoder means … and other structural features that carry out the invented process.	directed to a device that performs the encoding process thus fall into machine category
Claim 15 read as: A <u>storage medium</u> having stored thereon a signal with embedded supplemental data	directed to a storage (device) holding the resulting signal, which falls into manufacture statutory category[1]

---

[1] Asserted by the BPAI (Board of Patent Appeal and Interferences), which allowed claim 15.

The patent application (US 09/211,928) by Nuijten was brought to US Court of Appeals for Federal Circuit [Appeal No. 2006-1371] due to rejected claims by the USPTO. The invention was about digital watermark. Digital watermarking scheme is to embed additional data in a signal by encoding the original signal in such a way that the delta between original signal and encoded signal can only be detected by software but not obtrusively noticeable to a human being. The invention by Nuijten introduces a modified encoding scheme on existing watermark techniques such that the signal distortion introduced by delta is minimized.

The allowed groups of claims with the reasoning behind are listed in Table 5.2. While the reasoning behind the allowed claims are relatively straightforward for their subject matter patentability test, what is controversial is its claim 14 that reads as:

"A signal with embedded supplemental data, the signal being encoded in accordance with a given encoding process ...."

which is directed to a signal that is not easy to categorize into one of the statutory categories. The USPTO rejected claim 14 based on 35 USC 101 (patentable subject matter), and this rejection was appealed to the Federal Circuit court, which issued decision with two different opinions between two judges. The result and its rationale are summarized in Table 5.3.

As illustrated in the case study, the fundamental difference in opinions lies on the interpretation of what constitutes manufactures in the statutory category and whether it needs or need not be tangible.

The take home of this case study is how important the patentable subject matter is and how you might put your own invention under this test before you decide to file your application.

5.2.3 *Novelty*

The novelty of your invention is based upon what exists in prior arts and what is new in your invention. If at least one component/element of your system is new, you fulfill the novelty test.

Table 5.3 Court decisions in statutory category case study.

Decision	Rationale
USPTO decision: reject	35 USC 101: 1. Signal has no physical attributes, thus it is considered "abstract idea" 2. Falls into none of the statutory categories - signal is not reciting acts, thus not process - signal has no concrete tangible physical structure thus not a machine - signal is clearly not composition of matter - signal is not manufacture because manufacture requires a tangible object
Judge Gajarsa: affirmed the USPTO decision	1. Applicant argues that signal is connected to a physical form such that any signal needs to be conveyed by a physical carrier. Judge agrees with that line of thinking but pointed out the text of claims is not limited by any such specified physical medium. 2. Claims are not in any statutory category - signal claim does not cover act or series of acts thus not a process - no part of the signal is mechanical device thus not a machine - signal does not itself comprise tangible article or commodity, thus not manufacture (most difficult part) - signal is clearly not composition of matter
Judge Lynn: reversed the USPTO decision	1. Claim at issue is "new" and "useful" "manufacture" thus patentable under 35 USC 101. 2. Manufactures need not be tangible. Signal has physical form, signal has been given new form, quality or property by direct human action or by machine, anything made for use from raw or prepared materials is a manufacture.

Let us take a look at the exemplary invention. You are inventing a cordless phone, and it can be described in a pseudo claim structure:

1. A telephone base with a communication interface for attaching to a telephone wire;

2. A phone dialer;
3. A handset with microphone and speaker, whereby the handset can be moved away from the telephone base without connecting with a wire.

Imagine there was no cordless phone at the time of your invention. By examining your invention above, the telephone base and the phone dialer all exist in a conventional phone. The third item, however, is new because the traditional phone's handset cannot be moved away from the telephone base without a long wire. As above, at least one component in our invention is new; therefore, you satisfy the novelty test.

5.2.4   *Nonobviousness*

Obviousness is often used by the patent examiner to reject your claims based on one or more prior arts. When your claims are rejected on obviousness (also 35 USC 103), the examiner usually argues that your invention is an obvious improvement of the cited prior art, or obvious over a combination of multiple prior arts.

In the early stage of inventing process, especially before you decide to file your patent, you would not encounter having to argue about nonobviousness because there is no such Office Action yet. However, it will be to your own advantage if you can run a sniff test on nonobviousness for your invention.

Similar to novelty test, in nonobviousness test, you would need to compare your invention with related work, and determine whether your invention would be an obvious or inherited improvement from the prior art. What is obvious or inherited improvement? To be prudent, you need to ask yourself the following questions: After reading related prior art, do you think the inventor of the prior art or anyone skilled in the art and familiar with the prior art will easily extend the prior art and derive yours? Consider obviousness from patent examiner's perspective: is your invention an obvious combination of existing known elements?

Certainly, before a patent is examined, as an inventor, you would want to concentrate on the difference between your invention and the prior art you know of. You would want to be sure that such difference is not minor or nontechnical in order to reach the comfort level of moving ahead and filing your patent.

Finally, you can be prudent in running the patentability test on your invention, but make sure you do not throw out seemingly trivial yet great ideas.

5.3   Patenting Beyond Core Algorithms

Many scientists who used to develop scientific algorithms and file patents only on algorithms now shift to expanding their thinking in software applications and business methods. This may dramatically increase the value of their technologies and open up new business or enticing software applications that utilize those underlying technologies.

You may have invented an image compression algorithm for pictures. Have you thought about patenting and claiming beyond the algorithm, for instance, a digital camera that stores compressed captured images? You may have invented an algorithm to recognize characters from document images. Have you thought about expanding your scope to other applications such as license plate recognition, landmark detection from video scenes etc.? If you have invented a video matching algorithm for video database and retrieval, have you thought about expanding to searching video on a mobile device or camera, or searching video on the Internet?

To help expand the scope of your invention, brainstorm with colleagues and people who may benefit from your invention. Come up with applications that may utilize your invention and see whether you can also patent those real applications as software or business methods. A lot of times those patents may not be overlooked as they may turn out to be more valuable than patenting the core algorithm alone.

5.4   Innovation Harvesting

Innovation harvesting is an important step in the innovation stage. Instead of invention impromptu, having a patent strategy allows you to plan ahead and systematically cover various innovation opportunities. Such strategy and planning give you a picture where you are in the patent landscape and help you make business decisions as to what to file. In general, innovation harvesting consists of the following steps to be described in the remainder of this section.

5.4.1 *Patent Brainstorming*

Patent brainstorming is particularly useful in an industry environment when a company is looking into launching a new product and seeking as broad protection as possible. Patent brainstorming shall lead to a list of new ideas.

People have the tendency to limit their ideas to what they know best, what they have been working on or the product they are developing daily. The idea of brainstorming is to dig hard into any possible space in your creativity and find something that you have never thought before. The methodology in conducting a brainstorming session is to create an informal and relaxed atmosphere. The day to day working place may not be a good place to conduct brainstorming for the above obvious reason.

Although patent brainstorming should run in an informal atmosphere, preparedness, agenda, focus and positive altitude are much needed in order to make it successful.

Years ago I have run a brand new company project on handheld interactive TV. We only had a conceptual product in mind at the time without a good array of applications. While crystallizing the product feature with business people in product divisions and engineers in various technical sectors, we launched a group brainstorming session. Some of the tips and key steps in making our brainstorming successful are listed below.

1. Participants: To think outside the box you would need a group of people with wide range of background. Do not limit your participants only to people in your team or people who are going to be involved in the project. Invite researchers, product division people, business people, receptionist, wives, mothers etc. You may be wondering why you invite people who have no technical background. Remember we

just talked in the previous section about patenting beyond algorithms as patents covering application concepts or business methods are often more important in getting a broad IP protection. You would definitely want to invite your targeted end users to help you create more exciting applications that can utilize your underlying technologies and expertise.

2. Preparedness: Brainstorming is an interactive experience. It often involves people tossing around ideas, one producing an idea with the stimulation of another. To coordinate such team work, the moderator needs to have a list of things to cover in order to make sure the brainstorming session covers key aspects of the product-to-be-invented. Take the handheld interactive TV device, for example, we have laid out three key areas that need to be covered at the brainstorming session:

    a. Handheld applications in connection with TV
    b. Channels for data download from providers to the device
    c. Channels for data upload from the device to providers

Everyone was given the main theme and key areas and let think of what they would like our target device be able to do to enhance their TV watching experience and everyday life around it. Each participant should be prepared before coming to the brainstorming session.

3. Agenda: The moderator should develop an agenda in advance to make sure the brainstorming is going in the right direction. Some tips in planning are:

    a. Scheduling: Brainstorming can be split into different sessions. For example, the first one can be at top levels with collection of application ideas, features of the products etc. The second one can be more technical on any new technological advancement aiming to enable the new applications collected from the first session. Different groups of people can be invited into different sessions.

    b. Timing and note taking: The moderator (or a designated person) should keep track of time to make sure there are enough break sessions, and keep notes of what have been discussed and who has contributed to the discussion.

4. Action item: Each brainstorming session should generate a list of innovation ideas and each should have action items. The moderator can review the results from the brainstorming session, combine similar ideas, categorize them into different groups and assign people who contributed originally at the brainstorming session to take it to the next step, which will be described below.

5. Positive attitude: Last but not the least, positive attitude is a must for a brainstorming session to succeed. At the brainstorming session, it is not the goal for people to criticize each other, but rather to help stimulate the creative environment that one can stimulate the thinking of another. There will be steps to filter all ideas, but not at the time of brainstorming. As we all try to create vision for future products and innovations, prematurely killing an idea too early may hinder such creation process.

5.4.2   *Prior Art Search and Market Analysis*

Once you have generated groups of innovative ideas, this step is to refine your strength in the technology landscape, examine potential competitors and companies having overlapping technologies. A preliminary prior art search and market analysis will be required in the follow up of the brainstorming session. This inevitably shifts the burden to the inventors.

Again, the strategy described in this section is more oriented towards initial innovation stage, in which you are attempting to discover new "loop holes" in the market and patent landscape, which will be described in more detail.

As the result of prior art search and market analysis, ideas generated from the brainstorming session will be ranked. Ideas that are ranked at the top may need more iterations of brainstorming in a similar fashion to further flesh out more details including sketches, card board design and mock-ups, and how they are going to be enabled etc.

5.5   Patent Landscaping

Patent landscaping refers to a process of looking at broader trends related to patents such as if patent activity for a given area is increasing/

decreasing, the trend of the number of patents issued to competitors etc. A patent landscape is used to understand your patent portfolio, by showing the strength and weakness in the entire technology map. The strength is where there are relative fewer patents identified in your prior art search and market analysis stage. The weakness is where there are relatively more relevant patents or products identified.

There is no standard definition of patent landscape or process how patent landscaping should be conducted. This section intends to only scratch the surface and give you some ideas on what concrete elements are usually involved in patent landscaping.

What are Data Sources?

The primary data for patent landscaping requires no special data collection. It is simply coming from your patent search. The raw data you need to collect may include the following:

1. Total number of relevant issued patents found
2. Total number of relevant published patent applications found
3. Total number of your own patents and published applications
4. All key bibliographical data for each patent including:
    a. Title/abstract
    b. Inventor's name and geographical location (place of residence)
    c. Assignee's name
    d. Filing date
    e. Claims

The determination on the relevancy of patents may be based upon a perusal of title and abstract of each patent from your patent search. Depending on the level of details of the analysis to be done, the selection of relevant patents can be done differently. If you are only intending to get a rough idea of the trend of a general technology, counting all patents in a specific class may suffice. If you are assessing your risk associated with a specific product you are developing, a cursory review of title and abstract will be necessary.

What are You Looking For?

From the patent landscaping process, many IP professionals are now seeking to answer broader technology intelligence questions such as:

1. "How is my IP positioned in this market?" – To answer this question, you will compare the number of relevant patents from your competitors and the number of your own patents. What are the "patent share" between you and your competitors? At this level the larger number of patents should give indications of a stronger portfolio.
2. "Who are my small/large technology competitors?" – You will identify your competitors from the assignee names of relevant patents you find from your patent search.
3. "What is the trend of R&D activity of a competitor?" – You will observe the number of published patent publications per year from your competitor. You may see the trend of this number increasing/decreasing over a timeline that reflects their R&D effort.
4. "Are there any prolific key inventors in a competitor?" – For each of your competitor, you may look into inventor names of all related patents from this competitor and see which inventor has the most patents.
5. "Are there any potential threats in the technology area I'm pursuing?" – You will need to find out the number of relevant patents from your competitor, which reflects the potential threats for your presence in the market.
6. "Who would be a partner candidate or in/out license target?" – You will compare your weakness with your competitors' portfolio to identify potential partner company whom you may need to license-in to strengthen your portfolio or obtain freedom of action for your products. Compare your strength with competitors to identify perspective license-out target companies who might be interested in taking a license of your technology.

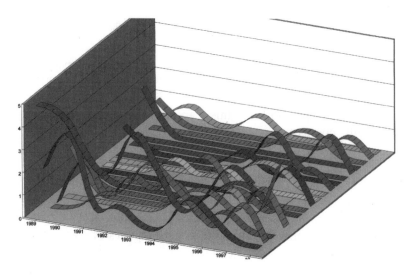

Fig. 5.2 The number of patent applications per year by competitor.

There are many ways of answering the above fundamental questions, either in a table, in a graph or in a pie chart etc. Figure 5.2 illustrates an exemplary chart as the result of patent landscaping process[2]. It shows inventive activities among competitors (represented by different ribbons) in a specific technology area in pharmaceutical. The variation of the number of filings each year reflects the patent activities thus R&D effort along the timeline. As shown, there are significantly more competitors in the research area under study during 1994 and 1997 in comparison to late 80's or early 90's when there are only a few major players.

Another example of patent landscaping is illustrated in Fig. 5.3, in which a technology clustering from a company's imaging portfolio is shown using the ThemeMap feature of Aureka. The concentration of various technologies helps identify the strength and weakness of the portfolio.

---

[2] Courtesy of Pharmaceutical Patent Attorneys, LLC. The full article can be found at: Mark Pohl, "Patent Landscaping Studies: Their Use in Strategic Research Planning", Pharmaceutical News, vol. 9, pp. 127–135 (2002).

From patent landscaping, you should be able to identify the strength and weakness of your portfolio, understand your competitors, uncover any "loop holes" in the technology area that have not been fully developed and be able to recommend your next action how and where to strengthen your portfolio.

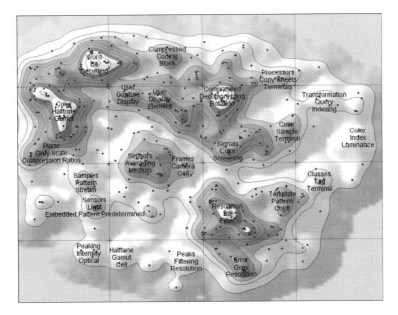

Fig. 5.3 A snapshot of ThemeMap tool from Aureka.

5.6   Making Filing Decisions

Finally, it is time to make strategic recommendation or decide what disclosure should file as a patent application. The main considerations will be listed and explained below.

1. How essential is the technology to your business and the industry?
2. What patent rights will you be getting from each patent-to-file (idea)?
3. Market consideration (international filing).
4. Budget constraint.

Essentiality

You need to be clear how good the invented technology is. Is it solving a long felt need? Is it essential to your product and business? Is it essential to the industry? Without such invented technology, can your product still survive and differentiate from your competitors?

Patent Rights

A granted patent only gives you rights to exclude others from making your invention. Before you file your own patent, you may want to think how much exclusive rights your invention (supposedly it will be granted) is going to give you and whether it is sufficient for you to patent it.

To compare your innovative concepts with prior arts or existing systems, there are two key aspects you will need to examine with respect to your perspective exclusive rights:

1. Claim breadth: the broadness of claims. If you are inventing a device or system that has never existed before, you are likely to get a broad claim. On the other hand, if you are making incremental improvement on existing systems, it will be difficult to obtain a broad claim.
2. Invent-around: how easy it is to work around your invention and still achieve the same functionality. Invent-around is a key to measure the effectiveness of your exclusive right to exclude someone from practicing your invention. If your invention is easy to circumvent, it may not give you a strong protection even if it is a sounding technology. On the other hand, if your invention is hard to get around, it may still have good business application and strong legal enforceable rights even if it is not a scientific breakthrough.

After the "sniffing" test for your invention, you shall have a good idea how strong a claim and exclusive rights you may get. Also, in terms of pyramid portfolio strategy as explained in Chapter 2, think of at what level your new invention is going to be.

Market Consideration

A patent only gives you protection in the country it is granted. If you have a U.S. patent and are selling your product in the U.S., you are protected. However, if you are selling the same product in Japan, you would need to have a corresponding Japanese patent (foreign counterpart) in order to be protected in that country.

While it is often not feasible to file in every single country for every single patent, it is important to decide which markets (countries) are likely to be viable to deploy your invention and file patents. This is often driven by the company's business strategy and future product roadmap.

The final result from your idea to innovation harvesting process discussed in this chapter is going to be a prioritized list of patent disclosures from high to low, and sorted by market. You need to discuss with legal counsel and related business division people, consider budget constraints and eventually finalize which disclosure to file, and which to file international application (PCT) or domestic application.

Chapter 6

Preparations Before Filing

Before we dive into patent filing, let us spend a moment discussing several fundamentals you need to be aware of in patent protection. You will be better prepared to file your own patents.

6.1 Lab Book: To Document Your Invention

Normally, the priority date of an invention goes by their filing date (or the early filing date of its parent patent of which it claims the benefits). However, by the U.S. patent law, the priority date of an invention goes by the date when the invention was conceived, not when it was filed. Section 3.4 discusses priority date and scenarios when an invention's conception date is critical. The key to successfully obtaining early priority date when needed is to save every piece of evidence during the course of your invention.

Corroboration has been applied to patent law regarding invention in the case law, in which "an inventor's testimony respecting facts surrounding a claim of derivation or priority of invention cannot, standing alone, rise to the level of clear and convincing proof". Evidence needs to be provided. The evidence can be found sometimes in the inventor's notes, computer programs or experimental procedures. Although these notes are normally kept for inventor's own purposes, they can sometimes become critical information in determining the priority date or proving the true inventorship of the invention.

The lab book, or the invention book, is considered the most important tool in recording your ideas. It provides acceptable evidence to prove your ownership of the invention. The lab book, traditionally a bound paper book, keeps your ideas, inventions, sketches and details organized. It is important to date any contents that go in there, and have someone witness it each time you do so.

With the advancement of computer systems and low cost of storage media, you are advised to keep all raw information (even ideas before you discuss with your group) in an organized way so they can be quickly located if needed. In addition, if you are experimenting and developing a prototype for your invention, you are advised to save all receipts when you buy materials. Again, time stamp (either electronically, or printed or digitally signed with time stamp) is critical in maintaining your records.

6.2 Priority Date

The priority date is crucial to the success of your patent. The earlier the priority date of a patent is, the more references can be disqualified as prior art, and the more likely your claims can be obtained. The rule of thumb is to file as early as possible. Practically, you should be aware of the following tips.

6.2.1 *File Provisional*

If you are not ready to file your applications, file provisional. Provisional filing has minimal requirements. You do not need claims. Drawings do not need to be formal. Once you file provisional application, you have a 12-month grace period to file your nonprovisional application and still can claim the benefit of provisional filing date.

What is important in filing provisional is to gather as much material as possible without foreseeing any changes on your technical contents. If you later introduce a new concept in your nonprovisional, it will not claim the benefit of the early filing date of your provisional. Therefore, you are not advised to rush your disclosure or file a "thin" provisional which is not technically ready. The 12-month grace period is not meant to let you perfect your invention. Rather, it gives you time to perfect your applications, prepare your drawings and complete your claims.

You may file as many provisional applications as you desire, and later combine them into one nonprovisional application. Also, the provisional application gives you an early priority date, but does not let you lose patent life since the life of a patent is calculated from when the nonprovisional application is filed.

6.2.2   *File Early*

Although the U.S. patent law goes with "first-to-conceive" policy, to prove the early conceiving date of your invention, extra steps and time will be needed. Furthermore, while there is an ongoing debate in the House and Senate on patent reform, the "first-to-conceive" policy may be nullified. Your best bet is to file as early as possible.

6.2.3   *File Before You Publish or Make Public Speech*

Many researchers have interests in both patenting and writing academic papers. If you publish first then file a patent, extreme precautions need to be made.

This relates to the "statutory bar date" or "critical date" upon which a prior art is determined whether it is eligible to be included in the examination. Such statutory bar date is defined as one year preceding the patent filing date[1], where a patent will be denied because "the invention was patented or described in a printed publication in this or a foreign country or in public use or on sale in this country, more than one year prior to the date the application for patent in the United States." Therefore, you are allowed to publish your invention or make public use of your invention first, then file a patent within 12 months, after which your own publication or public use will bar against yourself in obtaining a patent.

---

[1] Patent law 35 USC 102(b).

However, the 12-month grace period is unique in the U.S. patent system, whereas under the European regime there is no grace period at all. Under Japanese system, only six-month grace period is granted on inventor's own activities prior to the filing. For this reason, it is strongly suggested that you file a patent before you intend to publish a paper or make any public speeches about your invention because doing otherwise may seriously risk your chance of obtaining patents in foreign countries.

6.3 Prior Art and Statutory Bar Against Your Application

In normal prosecution, examiners commonly reject your claims at the first Office Action by citing one or more prior arts, which can be granted patents, published patent applications or other public publications including conference and journal articles, trade show brochures etc. The examiner may also reject your claims by public use. For example, the invention may have been used or demonstrated in public.

The general rule is that if anything listed above predates your application it may bar your own application from being granted. However, there are two scenarios that your application may not be barred:

1. Public use and public known information are only applicable in the U.S. Because U.S. patents only give you legal rights in U.S. market, any existing and known public use of your invention in foreign countries is not considered a statutory bar against your application.
2. There is a statutory bar date, which is the 12-month grace period before the filing date of your application. If the cited prior art occurs within the 12-month grace period, and you have evidence to show that your invention was conceived before the prior art, you may "swear back" of your own priority date in order for the USPTO to disqualify the prior art.

The statutory bar date, qualification of prior art and "swear back" of priority date will be further discussed in Chapter 9. At this point, you need to be aware that even you have known some prior art or public information may be in the way of getting your patent, you still have a couple of options depending on the types, country and date of the prior art.

At last, remember to file provisional application as soon as your invention is conceived, without possible detrimental delay. The fee is minimal, but you will be able to claim an early priority date without the hassle required for "swear back" of date.

6.4   Working with Attorney

Although many scientists and engineers wish they had their own choice in selecting which attorney to work with, many working in a large corporation or a university have no choices since the institution generally contracts out one or several attorney firms to handle their filings. This system, which is common in many industries and organizations, do present challenges. This section talks about the drawback of the system, and suggests how to get around.

The presented challenges in existing patent filing system are:

1. Attorneys' hours are very expensive. Because of billable hours they have to meet, attorneys seldom have time for interactions or face-to-face meetings with inventors.
2. Billing is directly sent to the company's or university's intellectual property office; inventors have no information and is unable to direct their efforts to where they may get the most help for the buck.
3. Most organizations contract with attorneys in law firms, whose primary role is patent filing and litigation. Patent licensing and sales, on the other hand, are primarily handled by another industry. Therefore, the integrity of patent specification and claims are not fully maximized at patent filing stage. There are different interests between inventor/patent owners and attorneys; and there is often a lack of linkage to the economic value of a patent at its filing stage.
4. Attorney's turn over or shifting of priorities within a law firm occurs very often, which causes transition of attorneys for the same case. There is almost no handover of work when the work is shifted from one attorney to another. It is not uncommon in a law firm that an attorney is responding an Office Action for a case filed by another

attorney. The learning curve in familiarizing the subject matter for the new attorney may have impact on the quality of claims that may be obtained.

Although working with attorney presents challenges, there are some tactics you may use in order to get the most out of the system:

1. Prepare ideas, clear thoughts, background information, enablement and documentations etc. Do not expect attorneys to invent for you. You have to give them the "meat" instead of a simple sketch on a napkin. An attorney's job is not to fill in the "meat" for you, but rather to package and present your invention in a way that your patent rights can be maximally obtained.
2. Request meetings and interactions particularly before the first draft is finished, to ensure your inventive concepts are well understood by your attorney.
3. Provide editable electronic version as much as possible to save your attorney's time (i.e. to save your money too). You would certainly not want to pay them high dollars just to spend time on converting your sketch drawings into electronic format.
4. Provide references and tutorials for your attorney to understand the field and the problem you are trying to solve. This effort of coaching will bring benefits later on.
5. It is important that the attorney not only understands your invention, but also is able to conceptualize how broad your technology can go. Make sure he understands your invention by asking him questions.
6. During patent prosecution, it is extremely important to consult an attorney on correspondence to Office Actions. Make sure you understand the issues raised by the examiner, and attorney's arguments are right on the issue. Some not-on-the-point arguments may cause the closing of the case (final rejection) and lost of time in the prosecution. It will cost more to file a continuation application to resume the case.

6.5   Filing it Yourself

If you are an independent inventor, you may have the choice of filing it yourself in order to save money. There are numerous books teaching you how to patent it yourself. The objective of this section is not to teach you how to patent it yourself and handle the USPTO matters, but rather give you some tips and pitfalls in patent filing should you choose to do it yourself.

It is important to realize that the measure of success is not to simply get a patent granted, but to look at what kind of claims can be allowed as claims are the only legal rights you will be entitled to. This is particularly true for individual inventors who have limited budget and have chosen to patent themselves.

When you patent yourself, a few things need to be paid more attention.

1. Patentability test. Because you are under budget constraint, you would not want to spend all your time and efforts on filing your application only to find out later that your idea has already been public information or patented by someone else. You need to do your research on finding relevant patents and make sure you are confident that your invention is novel and nonobvious, as described in the preceding chapter.
2. Clear specification. Just as you would write an academic paper, describe clearly how your system works. Do not be shy disclosing the greatest part of your invention as if you are giving out your trade secret. As mentioned before, best mode is required by the patent law. To add broader protection to your invention, you are encouraged to disclose alternative embodiments – i.e. to cover as many different ways as possible. And a suggestion to making your patent strong is to disclose your best mode but not to disclose what, amongst the multiple modes of operation, is the best mode.
3. Patent claims. Patent claims are the heart of your patent. You need to make your best effort to make sure:
   a. All claim languages are supported in your specification.
   b. Claims are broadened to the best you can from what is described in the specification.

Furthermore, Chapter 7 will also provide you with many tips and pitfalls in patenting that will help you write a quality patent application.

6.6 Trade-off Solution

6.6.1 *Patent Agent or Patent Attorney*

Patent law firms used to have the advantages of owning proprietary tools to do an efficient patent search and having easy access to the USPTO patent search room. This was particularly so for many patent attorneys around Washington D.C. area due to their proximity to the USPTO. This advantage, however, is diminishing with the advent of the Internet and the emergence of readily available free tools and patent databases from the USPTO and third parties.

If you decide to hire a professional, patent filing and prosecution can be done by either an attorney or a patent agent. Many people have the misconception that only patent attorney can do the filing and a patent agent's work has to be approved by a patent attorney. The fact is that both patent attorneys and patent agents have to pass the same USPTO sanctioned patent bar exam in order to practice at the USPTO. A patent agent can fully represent you in any patent filing and prosecution at the USPTO.

The main difference between a patent attorney and a patent agent is that a patent attorney can represent a client in a court for patent litigation whereas a patent agent cannot. On the other hand, in a large law firm, attorneys are mostly functionally divided into groups. A patent attorney working on patent filing may not have had any opportunity working on patent litigation and appeared in a court, and it is likely so. Therefore, the difference between patent attorney and patent agent becomes less important as far as patent filing and prosecution is concerned. The important consideration in choosing your service provider is how experienced the patent attorney or agent is.

There are some online services for patent filing at low prices. They ask you to simply submit your specification online and they will complete the application for you. One suggestion regarding these services is not to fall into the trap of cheap price. You will not know who or which patent agent/attorney they are using, and how they can comprehend your invention by simply reading your specification.

In summary, the critical things you need to pay attention when selecting a professional to do your filing are primarily the following:

1. Experience of your attorney or agent in both legal and technical field.
2. Interactions you are getting during the service. As previously stated in this chapter, interaction with the attorney/agent is very important for patent filing and prosecution. If the attorney or agent does not give you enough time for interaction, consider another one.
3. Any licensing, assertion or litigation background of the same attorney or agent will give you some forward thinking on your application and claims.
4. Fees.

6.6.2   *Combination of Patenting Yourself and Professional Service*

Many independent inventors have tried to file patent themselves, and ended up with seeking professional service at the end. Practically, when an inventor receives the first Office Action that rejects all of their claims, he often seeks professional service immediately.

A hybrid and more affordable way to filing would be to prepare the patent application yourself as much as you can and ask a professional (patent attorney or agent) to finalize it. It is also recommended to ask a professional to handle your Office Action matters during patent prosecution.

For the hybrid model, it is critically important for you to write a clear and thorough specification. Even if you delegate the entire filing to a professional, you are still encouraged to do so. The advantage of doing this is twofold:

1. Writing the specification by yourself (just as if you are writing a technical report) gives you a chance to think through every detail how your invention is going to be enabled and how the system works.

2. A clear specification will allow the professional working on your case to comprehend quickly and save their time and your money in the end.

To split the work, you may use a professional to help you with what you cannot do by yourself due to lack of training or experience. Examples are:

1. Integrity of the specification. You have followed the patent-it-yourself books to write your specification. You should have a professional review it and add any necessary support language in order to obtain maximum space in your claim.
2. Claims. Have this handled by a patent attorney or agent. However, you need to have enough interaction with her to make sure she comprehends your invention well and has "stretched" as much as possible to reach reasonable broad claims. When I was working with attorneys, I often asked them how they were going to draft the independent claims even before they did it. This ensures their complete understanding of the scope of the invention while I can get a clear picture of what kind of claim space I am going to get from their answer. With such mutual understanding and confidence, I know the claims will come out strong.
3. Office Action response. It is better to leave this to a professional because you only have limited opportunities of rebuttal. After the second rejection, the examiner usually issues a final Office Action, which will leave further limited choices and it will be costly to request continuation of the examination. Work closely with the professional at each Office Action to reach your agreement how you determine to respond: whether to argue or narrow down claims to overcome any prior arts that may be cited by the examiner.

To conclude this chapter, I strongly recommend you to get involved in the patent filing stage particularly help maintaining high quality of the specification as any noneditorial change will be considered new matter and therefore lose its priority date. Never sketch your idea on a napkin and ask the attorney/agent to draft the rest of the application for you. Without writing your first cut of the specification yourself, you would not have thought through how the entire invention works and counting on attorney to fill in that "hole" will make your invention much vulnerable.

Chapter 7

Essentials in Patent Filing

So now you have sorted the ideas and come up with the final list of innovations to file. You are confident with your decision in terms of both market potential and patentability through your preliminary preparation work. The next important step is to put your innovation into a patent application and claim your property. Methods to claiming your property are not only determined by how the claims are written, but also by the integrity of your entire patent application, whose quality directly affects the economic value of your patent.

This chapter talks about essentials in filing a patent application and how you should use your resources at this stage.

7.1 Structural Parts of a Patent and Their Purposes

Various structural parts of a patent have been explained in Section 4.1. Each structural part has its own purpose, yet they are not equally important particularly in terms of claiming the legal rights of the patent owner. This section explains each basic structural part of a patent and its purpose. This will particularly benefit people who are new to the patent system.

7.1.1 *Title*

Title gives a brief description of the invention, and is required to be less than 500 characters. It should be technically accurate and descriptive. As described in MPEP [1], it is also imperative that no words such as "improvement", "improved" be used as they are vague and do not suggest any technical characteristics of the invention. Title bears no legal effect. Ideally, the title should be indications of the invention to which claims are directed. A common problem for the title is it often intends to be too broad or vague and becomes less descriptive such as "An image processing apparatus", "A computer system" etc. During patent prosecution, the examiner may suggest a new title to make it more compliant with the USPTO guideline.

7.1.2   *Abstract*

As described in MPEP, "the abstract in an application filed under 35 U.S.C. 111 may not exceed 150 words in length. The purpose of the abstract is to enable the United States Patent and Trademark Office and the public generally to determine quickly from a cursory inspection the nature and gist of the technical disclosure."[2] For best practice, it is often suggested that abstract is written at the end of the application drafting process to make sure it truly reflects the technical nature of the invention. However, it is inevitable that abstract becomes stale after several iterations of Office Action, claim amendment etc. that the abstract may end up being broader than what is actually claimed in the invention.

Whether an abstract is broader than what is actually claimed bears no legal responsibility from the inventor. As a matter of fact, many attorneys prefer that way to make sure there is no evidence that the spirit of the invention is being unnecessarily narrowed anywhere in the specification in any way.

7.1.3   *Background of the Invention*

The background of the invention often consists of two parts: The field of invention and the description of related patents.

---

[1] MPEP Section 606.
[2] MPEP Section 608.1.

The field of invention is usually a statement of the art or field to which the invention pertains. This statement may include a paraphrasing of the applicable U.S. patent classification definitions and should be directed to the subject matter of the claimed invention. For example, in the field of invention for the exemplary patent in Section 4.1, it reads: "The present invention relates generally to the control of audio, video and multimedia equipment". It is pretty broad at this level. Optionally, as in this patent, more particulars are added: "More particularly, the invention relates to an on-screen user interface for interacting with audio, video and multimedia components using a remote control apparatus having a digitized writing surface for entry of hand-drawn instructions by the user".

The second part of the Background of the Invention should list, where appropriate, the prior arts and describes their shortcoming and what problems those prior arts cannot solve, yet being solved by the current invention. As much as the USPTO or Judges would want every inventor to include this section in their patent specification in order to give readers a clear idea what their invention is about, in practice, many people would want to leave this information out intentionally to avoid any adverse effect on their defensive ability should their patent be challenged at the court.

7.1.4 *Brief Summary of the Invention*

The brief summary of the invention is similar to abstract but gives more details of the subject matter of the invention and what the claims have been directed to. If there are multiple embodiments in the invention, they should be clearly summarized in this section.

Brief summary of the invention is often an entry point for any reader to easily grasp the concept of the invention and should be written in a natural language just like any technical papers. In reality, some people seem to do it differently. Two examples are shown in Figs. 7.1 and 7.2, respectively.

> The present invention takes a fresh approach to the problem. Although the hand-held remote with push buttons may still be used, the present invention provides a digitizing writing surface through which the user may enter hand-drawn instructions. These instructions can be handwritten text, symbols or even pictures, all of which are written to the digitized writing surface using a pen or stylus. Such a means for controlling the system and providing input appeals to a broader range of users than does a conventional keyboard. Through the mechanism of providing hand-drawn instructions, complex systems can be controlled with ease.

Fig. 7.1 An exemplary summary of the invention.

Figure 7.1 illustrates a paragraph of the summary of the invention from one patent shown earlier in Chapter 4. The summary of the invention clearly describes the essence of the invention: it employs a stylus on a hand-held remote control and uses hand-drawn instructions to control complex video systems.

> In accordance with one aspect of the present invention, a graphic editing system is provided which comprises a data interface surface having identifiable coordinates, a first application program including means for displaying data on said surface, first means interacting with said surface for controlling said first application and for modifying said data displayed on said surface, second means responsive to operation of said first means for storing coordinates of said interaction and for suspending control of said first application program, and third means responsive to subsequent interaction of said first means with said data surface at said coordinates for selectively enabling execution, clarification and cancellation of said control of said first application.

Fig. 7.2 Another example of summary of the invention.

Figure 7.2 shows another example of the summary of the invention, which is just the rewording of claims and is extremely difficult to read without any deeper knowledge of claim language. It seems to give readers little information of what the patent is truly about. When comparing Fig. 7.2 to Fig. 7.1, both being excerpted from the Summary of the Invention of two different patents, they seem to be written in totally different languages.

For the counter example in Fig. 7.2, there are some legal rational for doing so. Some attorneys are concerned with making the summary of the invention unnecessarily narrow thus prefer using the same language as the claims. This method, however, is generally not welcome by readers in large, nor is it welcome by judges at the court (when handling patent litigation). Therefore, by all means you should write your summary of the invention in a plain natural language in order to benefit readers. When doing so, in order to address any potential legal concerns, you need to make sure the scope of the summary of the invention is not narrower than that of your broadest claim.

7.1.5 *Description of Drawings*

This section gives a simple list of drawings in the specification and the titles for each drawing. For the ease of the patent examiner and readers to better understand the subject matter, it is often necessary to illustrate by drawing where appropriate just like any scientific paper. In addition, any part that is cited in the specification should be labeled clearly in the drawing by a numeric part number.

7.1.6 *Detailed Specification of the Invention*

As the section title explains, all the details of the invention and any variations of implementations should be described in here, as if you are writing a technical report or scientific article. As the heart of the patent specification, this section should be paid most attention for several reasons:

1. A well-written patent should provide good enabling support of claims in the specification, as will be explained in the next section.
2. During patent prosecution, claims can be amended. However, once a patent application is filed, its specification cannot be changed (except corrections of obvious typo) as it will be considered introducing new matter. Any new matter will be deleted in patent examination or it

will be considered for a later priority date. Therefore, a well-written specification is extremely important.

7.1.7   *Claims*

Claims give you legal exclusive rights. The scope of claims, the market acceptance (usefulness) of the invention and the size of the market pertaining to affected market acceptance are primary driving factors of the economic value of a patent. You would want to claim as broad as possible to increase the size of affected market. However, during patent prosecution, your claims may be amended to narrow its scope in order to avoid prior arts that the examiner identifies, and at the end, your ultimate allowed claims may not be much of use at all due to its much narrowed scope than originally intended. Some tips in claim drafting will be covered in a separate section in this chapter.

7.1.8   *Prototype*

Experiments and prototypes are not required for a patent contrary to scientific papers. The requirement for a patent is that the invention should be a working system that allows an ordinary skilled in the art to be able to build it according to your specification. It is particularly to the advantages of software and business method patents for which a pseudo code or diagram can sufficiently enable the invention. For other types of patents, however, such as mechanical systems, composition of matters and biosciences patents, extensive experiments are often needed in order to make the system work (reduce to practice). For plant patent, a prototype is often required.

7.2   Specification and Claims

Specification cannot be changed once a patent is filed. It is, therefore, a high responsibility of the inventor to make sure the specification is correct and has a good foundation. Writing patent specification is similar to writing a technical report or a scientific paper from the technical point of view. It is important to express clearly in the specification the concept of the innovation and describe how the invention works. However, there are certain common mistakes seen in many patents that raise issues in future licensing or litigations. The following should be enforced in the specification.

7.2.1 *Clear Terminologies*

As required in MPEP[3], "The meaning of every term used in any of the claims should be apparent from the descriptive portion of the specification with clear disclosure as to its import... A term used in the claims may be given a special meaning in the description. ... This is necessary in order to insure certainty in construing the claims in the light of the specification".

As stated, an inventor does have freedom using any terms in the claims as long as he clearly defines the meaning of such terms in the specification. A well-written patent should fulfill this requirement. Furthermore, should the inventor make amendment of claims during patent prosecution, he should make sure that any new limiting languages/terms to be added to the amendment of claims should already have clear support in the specification.

Should ambiguity arise in later construing of claims due to unclear definition of claim terms in the specification, people may either take advantage of using the narrowest possible interpretation at the time the invention was made if it was a common terminology, or invalidate claims for lack of written description support.

7.2.2 *Enablement*

As stated in MPEP[4], "A disclosure in an application, to be complete, must contain such description and details as to enable any person skilled in the art or science to which the invention pertains to make and use the invention as of its filing date".

---

[3] MPEP 608.01 (o).

[4] MPEP 608.01(p).

The purpose of patent specification is to teach the ordinary skilled in the art to build the same invention. It is, therefore, a requirement of the specification to describe how the invention works considering that such invention shall be re-built by someone else purely based on such writing. This is often the key difference between a patent and an academic paper, in latter case people were mostly interested in the idea and experimental results to prove theoretic hypothesis; whereas in patent specification, much more details are needed to teach people how to implement the system.

A new idea alone does not equal to an invention since an invention requires enablement for what are claimed. As previously discussed, without much thought put into the enablement of the invention from inventors, a patent cannot certainly be of good quality.

7.2.3   *Alternative Embodiments*

As discussed in Chapter 4, alternative embodiments in a patent specification provide variations or different systems around the invention. Experts think that filing applications disclosing only a single embodiment is risky as single embodiment disclosures in United States patents are often the cause of broad claims being either narrowly interpreted or held invalid for lack of written description support.

For example, in case law Inpro II Licensing vs. T-Mobile USA, the term "host interface" in claims directed to a PDA that interfaces with a host computer was construed to be limited to "a direct parallel bus interface" as the judge concluded "the only host interface described in the specification is a direct parallel bus interface". As a result, the Blackberry PDAs, which use serial bus interface are not infringing.

Hypothetically, if you describe your invention of a smart remote control device communicating with your home entertainment system via infrared for it is the most feasible wireless link, you should also mention using other means of communications for achieving the same goal such as Bluetooth or Internet even it is not being used now. This can easily extend the scope of your invention.

7.2.4   *Best Mode*

As discussed in Sections 2.5 and 3.9, a patent needs to disclose its best mode as required by law. This is almost like giving up your secret. On the other hand, it is the only way to give you protection on your true invention. You should not fool people around by disclosing nonbest mode in the patent specification and at the same time implement your best mode in your products. There are several reasons you should not hide your best mode:

1. It is required by law. Once people find out you were knowledgeable of your best mode at the time your application was filed yet you did not disclose your best mode, your patent can be invalidated.
2. Disclosing your best mode is the only way to truly protect the invention of your most interest. If you intend to hide your secret (best mode), you are not actually seeking any protection and you should not file patent in the first place.
3. Not disclosing your best mode will make your patent vulnerable. Anyone who figured out your "secret" can either patent it themselves or freely use it even if you pre-date them.

7.2.5   *Best Mode is Not the Only Mode*

Very often, you would not want to limit your patent to your best mode at the time of filing for disclosing your best mode only may make your patent unnecessarily narrow.

A patent is good for 20 years. Your patent may not be useful or accepted by the market immediately after it is granted, but this situation may change within the 20 years of its life span. Your patent may become useful and widely accepted at its 15th year, which you may not be able to predict at the time of your invention. The strategy is to make your invention as expandable as possible from your core concept and disclose multiple embodiments how your invention can operate in different modes.

If you are concerned with giving out your secret by disclosing your best mode, the tip on how to "hide" your little secret is to disclose the best mode mingled with all other modes in multiple embodiments but not identifying what is your best mode. Although you are required by law to disclose your best mode, you are not required to identify what is your best mode in the specification. Such practice can often avoid being unnecessarily narrow about what you are entitled to claim, as one of your alternative embodiments may become the best mode some years down the road and you will still be able to claim then.

Last, try to avoid using words like "must", "only", "preferably" etc. so you are not stuck with any embodiments or limiting the scope of your invention.

7.3   Citing Other People's Works — Citations

7.3.1   *Backward Citation*

An inventor needs to fulfill his/her duty of disclosing related work, either patent, published publications or any other information. As previously introduced, the tool for doing this is IDS — Information Disclosure Statement. References cited in IDS become part of so-called backward citation, and this information is always printed on the cover page of a patent. The number of patents being cited is the backward citation count.

As shown in Fig. 7.3, an example of backward citation is disclosed in the "Reference Cited" section on the cover page of the patent. Further as shown on the cover page, the backward citation also consists of other publications (nonpatents). The references in backward citation may be cited by both inventors and examiners, for the latter the reference is marked by asterisk.

7.3.2   *Forward Citation*

The forward citation, on the other hand, is when the reference patent has been cited by other patents that were filed thereafter. As the forward citation occurs after a patent is granted, there is no way this information can be included on the cover page of the patent. In addition, the forward citation can still grow as it may be cited by more new arts. If you search patent online, many patent databases, such as the USPTO patent database give you the forward citation metric, as shown in Fig. 7.4.

(12) **United States Patent**
Hunter

(10) Patent No.: **US 7,184,048 B2**
(45) Date of Patent: **Feb. 27, 2007**

(54) **SYSTEM AND METHOD FOR GENERATING AN ANIMATABLE CHARACTER**

(75) Inventor: **Kevin L. Hunter**, San Jose, CA (US)

(73) Assignee: **Electric Planet, Inc.**, Seattle, WA (US)

(*) Notice: Subject to any disclaimer, the term of this patent is extended or adjusted under 35 U.S.C. 154(b) by 449 days.

(21) Appl. No.: **10/045,662**

(22) Filed: **Oct. 18, 2001**

(65) **Prior Publication Data**

US 2002/0118198 A1   Aug. 29, 2002

Related U.S. Application Data

(63) Continuation of application No. 09/173,583, filed on Oct. 15, 1998, now Pat. No. 6,384,819.

(60) Provisional application No. 60/062,361, filed on Oct. 15, 1997.

(51) Int. Cl.
G06T 13/00   (2006.01)
G06T 15/70   (2006.01)

(52) U.S. Cl. **345/473**; 345/474; 345/475

(58) **Field of Classification Search** 345/418, 345/419, 420, 473, 423, 428, 430, 474, 475
See application file for complete search history.

(56) **References Cited**

U.S. PATENT DOCUMENTS

5,031,620 A * 7/1991 Oe 600/425
5,148,477 A   9/1992 Neely et al. 382/6

5,454,043 A	9/1995	Freeman	382/168
5,548,659 A	8/1996	Okamoto	382/107
5,570,113 A	10/1996	Zetts	345/173
5,581,276 A	12/1996	Cipolla et al.	345/156
5,594,469 A	1/1997	Freeman et al.	345/158
5,991,057 A *	11/1999	Goldstein	359/32
6,141,463 A *	10/2000	Covell et al.	382/286
6,384,819 B1 *	5/2002	Hunter	345/418
6,906,713 B2 *	6/2005	Koshiro et al.	345/420

OTHER PUBLICATIONS

Huang, Chung-Lin; Wu, Ming-Shan, "A Model-based Complex Background Gesture Recognition System", 1996 IEEE International Conference on Systems, Man And Cybernetics. Information Intelligence and Systems Part vol. 1 p. 93-98.

* cited by examiner

Primary Examiner—Ulka Chauhan
Assistant Examiner—Roberta Prendergast
(74) *Attorney, Agent, or Firm*—Van Pelt, Yi & James LLP

(57)   **ABSTRACT**

A system and method are disclosed for generating an animatable object. A skeleton of the desired character is constructed by the user utilizing various predetermined components. These predetermined components include a various selection of rods and joints. The rods are static components which remain rigid during motion, while the various joints are moveable components. A static digitized image, for example, an image of the user, is utilized and a constructed skeleton is superimposed onto it. The desired object, such as the image of the user, can then be extracted from the background of the digital image and the resulting personal character can then be animated, for instance by selecting and dragging one of the hands with a mouse.

20 Claims, 10 Drawing Sheets

┌─ 300
Determine topology of skeleton

Fig. 7.3 Illustration of backward citation in patent cover page.

As illustrated in Fig. 7.4, a hyperlink "Referenced By" is provided in each of retrieved patent, and the click of this hyperlink gives a list of all patents which cited the reference patent. The total number of patents in this list is defined as forward citation count.

7.3.3   Tips in Citing Prior Arts

The strategy for handling IDS is that you must disclose what you know is relevant to your invention, but you should not disclose what is irrelevant. Over-citing references may not be a problem at all for scientific papers, as a matter of fact, it is often encouraged to cite as many work as possible to show thoroughness of literature research. Well, in patent application, citing too many references, particularly those not necessarily relevant, may not be beneficial to your patent examination.

In patent licensing world, both backward citation and forward citation are among many metrics that a patent will be evaluated. Very often, the forward citation count, i.e. how many times your patent has been cited by other people, is a good measure of the importance of the patent. As you can imagine, a patent having 50 forward citations being compared with a patent having zero forward citations may give a clear contrast that the former might be more important. You do not have much control on how

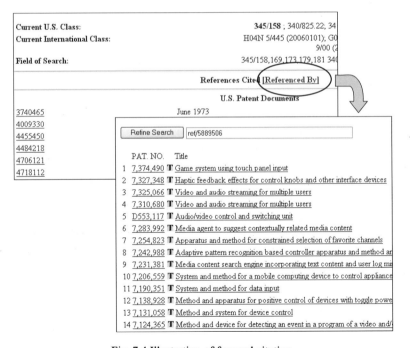

Fig. 7.4 Illustration of forward citation.

many people will cite your patent, the fact will speak itself. If your invention is indeed pioneering, essential, affecting much later work of other people, your patent will yield a higher forward citation count.

Although backward citation is not as an important metric as forward citation, it is related to forward citation in a way that your citing one's reference will become his forward citation. Therefore, you should not unnecessarily cite other people's work because you end up "glorifying" other people's patent unnecessarily. Furthermore, in many automated patent assessment tools, the backward citation count is an indicator of prior art risk. For example, if a patent has cited 50 references, it means there are a lot work that have been done prior to the invention, which may trigger more weight on the risk of prior art. The risk of prior art indicates the likelihood a patent claim can be invalidated.

In practice, cite highly relevant work in IDS only. If you do need to cite some work that is not critical to your invention such as tutorial materials, cite them in your own patent application specification in order to minimize unnecessary backward citation count.

7.4 What is Considered New Matter?

As briefly mentioned in Section 3.12, no new matter shall be allowed after a patent application is filed. This section attempts to give you an overview on what is considered to be new matter and what you need to do at the time of filing in order to avoid having to deal with any new matter issues at a later stage.

Anything related to the technical merits of the invention is considered new matter and will not be allowed after a patent is filed. The introduction of new matter may result in the shift of priority date and/or rejection of claims. Therefore, avoiding introduction of new matter is rather important during various stages of the patenting process including patent prosecution and any subsequent filing of continuation applications. These are further discussed in Table 7.1.

There are however some exceptions to new matter genre. These are:

1. Typographical errors which one skilled in the art would recognize.

2. Obvious corrections.
3. Rephrasing merely to make the invention more understandable.
4. Inheritance of functions.
5. Theory or advantages.
6. Incorporating text by reference.
7. Adding materials to the specification not disclosed in the specification but elsewhere (e.g. claims).

Table 7.1 New matter issues during patent filing and prosecution.

When	Remarks
Filing nonprovisional based on provisional	The spec can be changed, or combined with other provisional filings. New claims are to be added, but no introduction of new inventive concepts allowed.
During prosecution/examination	Amendment can be submitted to amend any part of the disclosure including drawing, but no new concepts/materials not introduced anywhere in the disclosure before should be added.
Filing continuation or continuation-in-part (CIP)	No new matter should be introduced in continuation application. New matter may be introduced in the CIP but the priority date of new matter or resulted claims will be the filing date of CIP.

These exceptions may give you some room to make some changes to your specification after your patent is filed. In reality, what exactly can be corrected or added without being considered to introduce new matter is not always clear. For example, what constitutes obvious correction? What is considered inheritance of functions and what is not? The answer to these questions in many times can be subjective. The best way to avoid all these issues later on is to always make your best effort to maintain the accuracy of your disclosure at the time of filing. Make sure all your claims are well supported in the specification or drawings.

Furthermore, although disclosure can be re-written in a non-provisional application claiming the benefits of a provisional application, it is important to include in the provisional application as many inventive concepts as possible particularly those elements necessary to enable the invention and those description pertaining to the best mode of the invention. This ensures you minimizing the risk of having to introduce new matter at a later stage.

7.5   Broaden and Diversify Your Claims

7.5.1   *Diversify your claims*

The statutory categories of invention mentioned in this book are somehow reflected in the claim types although it is not a one on one relation. For example, a process is often reflected in a process claim that defines steps or acts to be performed such as steps for a software widget to work correctly. Product claim, on the other hand, directs to machine, manufacture or compositions of matter[5]. Different types of claims have already been discussed in Section 4.5.

Utilize Different Types of Claims

To diversify your claims, you would like to make sure that the attorney or agent who is handling your application has put some thoughts into using different types in independent claims. This usually gives you better protection and leverage on how your patent can be used.

For example, a series of steps in software can be presented as a method claim. It can also be claimed as a system comprising various components, each representing a single step in the method claim. In this way, you may cover both software application as well as a device (system) running the software. If it is a software application on a cell phone, you have covered both software application and the cell phone, which gives you a larger market base for your patent.

Claim Novel Features in Multiple Ways

Another method of diversifying your claim is to describe a novel feature in multiple ways, each with similar scope to increase the likelihood of catching different types of infringers. Think about who might benefit your invention or part of the invention and try to draft claims to cover those scenarios.

---

[5] MPEP 2106.II.c.

The Amazon shopping patent ('411) that was illustrated in Section 4.5 is now further demystified in Table 7.2. Among the four independent claims: Claims 1 and 11 cover front end user interface/overall system aspect; Claim 6 covers client aspect of the system architecture and Claim 9 covers server aspects of the system architecture.

Table 7.2 Explanation of diversity of independent claims.

Independent Claims	Remarks
"1.A method of placing an order for an item comprising: under control of a client system, displaying information identifying the item; and in response to only a single action being performed, sending a request to order the item along with an identifier of a purchaser of the item to a server system; under control of a single-action ordering component of the server system, receiving the request; retrieving additional information previously stored for the purchaser identified by the identifier in the received request; and generating an order to purchase the requested item for the purchaser identified by the identifier in the received request using the retrieved additional information; and fulfilling the generated order to complete purchase of the item whereby the item is ordered without using a shopping cart ordering model."	A method claim describing steps required to order an item over the Internet with a SINGLE user action, without using shopping cart model.
6.A client system for ordering an item comprising: an identifier that identifies a customer; a display component for displaying information identifying the item; a single-action ordering component that in response to performance of only a single action, sends a request to a server system to order the identified item, the request including the identifier so that the server system can locate additional information needed to complete the order and so that the server system can fulfill the generated order to complete purchase of the item; and a shopping cart ordering component that in response to performance of an add-to-shopping-cart action, sends a request to the server system to add the item to a shopping cart.	A system claim describing a system from client's perspective for placing an item over the Internet. To infringe the claim, it requires to use an identifier (e.g. customer ID), a way for display item to the purchaser, a single-action for ordering, and a shopping cart.

Table 7.2 (Continued)

Independent Claims	Remarks
9.A server system for generating an order comprising: a shopping cart ordering component; and a single-action ordering component including: a data storage medium storing information for a plurality of users; a receiving component for receiving requests to order an item, a request including an indication of one of the plurality of users, the request being sent in response to only a single action being performed; and an order placement component that retrieves from the data storage medium information for the indicated user and that uses the retrieved information to place an order for the indicated user for the item; and an order fulfillment component that completes a purchase of the item in accordance with the order placed by the single-action ordering component.	A system claim describing a system from server's perspective for providing a platform for ordering items from the Internet in a single user action.
11.A method for ordering an item using a client system, the method comprising: displaying information identifying the item and displaying an indication of a single action that is to be performed to order the identified item; and in response to only the indicated single action being performed, sending to a server system a request to order the identified item whereby the item is ordered independently of a shopping cart model and the order is fulfilled to complete a purchase of the item.	A method claim similar to Claim 1, but broader, such that it does not limit how the single action is done (i.e. via the use of identifier of purchaser as in Claim 1).

As can be clearly understood, the claiming of novel features in different ways can be powerful in catching different types of infringers. For example, Claims 1 and 11 may catch eCommerce retailers; Claims 6 may cover eCommerce or mCommerce (mobile commerce) device manufacturers and Claim 9 may cover any network operator who provides server infrastructures.

7.5.2   Broaden Your Claims

In general although not in all cases, the shorter the claims are, the broader they are. A misconception, however, is that the more claims there are, the broader a patent is. The number of claims is important in securing diversified claim coverage, the length of each claim is equally important. The claim breadth refers to the quality of claim language in light of claim interpretation. In other words, it refers to how professional and solid the claim language is employed. Can it be expected to support a broad construction scope?

Specification can be thought of as an engineering drawing that allows people to build the same invention as you conceived. Claims, on the other hand, defines your legal rights that should be attempted to cover beyond your engineering drawing. Taking from your engineering drawing, there is a line of fuzziness, i.e. obvious thinking or inheritance. The objective of claim drafting is to be able to claim this fuzzy, obvious and inherited space, as illustrated in Fig. 7.5.

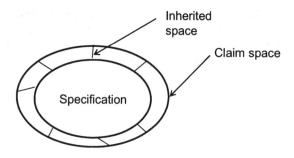

Fig. 7.5 Specification and claim scope.

In your specification, you should also look for any key limiting step/element or phrases that may significantly impact the use of claims and eliminate any limiting languages or optional steps in any independent claim in order to broaden it.

At last, when you have an idea and have figured out every single way that makes the system work, try to make claims as diverse as possible to cover both "trivial" and "difficult" techniques.

7.5.3 *Accuracy of Technical Content*

As mentioned before, any languages in the claims have to have support in the specification. Your claims might have gone through iterations of changes. You need to make sure to verify the accuracy of the technical content and revise your specification accordingly to support the broadened claims.

PART 3 Patent Prosecution and Post Granting

Chapter 8

Patent Prosecution

Patent prosecution is the most technical evaluation process but is often the process the inventor participates in the least. This procedure is basically the opportunity you are given to deal with the USPTO examiner to get your patent granted. It is usually handled by the attorney firm that filed your application. Because of billable hours and normally tight budgets for each case, attorneys usually deal with patent prosecution with little consultation from inventors.

This book strongly encourages inventors to get involved in the patent prosecution process to seek both the grant of the patent and the broadest claim. While rejection is a common decision in the first Office Action during patent prosecution, it pushes inventors to take another critical look at their own applications in the rebuttal of the rejection. This chapter talks about common issues you may encounter in patent prosecution and what options you should be aware of. The Office Action rebuttal and strategy itself is another topic and deserves its own attention in a separate chapter.

8.1   Prosecution History

Prosecution history, also called file wrapper or file history, is a record containing all correspondences between the USTPO and the applicant during the examination of an application. With very few exceptions, all the Office Actions you receive from the USPTO and all documents you submit to the USPTO will be contained in the prosecution history.

In June 2003, the USPTO has implemented image file wrapper (IFW) as part of its Patent Application Information Retrieval (PAIR) system.

Consequently, prosecution history for all patents filed after June 2003 is electronically available for free in the IFW of the USPTO public PAIR. The file history for older patents is available from numerous patent database providers for a nominal fee.

The prosecution history of a patent has been treated as serious as patent specification and claims during any patent transaction including licensing, sales, and litigation. For potential patent licensees or buyers, prosecution history is part of their due diligence material and is being used to augment the evaluation of a patent together with the reading of the patent.

A typical file history wrapper contains the following parts:

1. Application information including specification, claims, drawings, and information disclosure statement (IDS) in original filing.
2. Prosecution transaction history.
3. Application status.
4. Image file wrapper (IFW) contents including:
    - All Office Actions including rejections, notice of allowance etc.
    - Examiner's search strategy if any.
    - All of applicant's responses to Office Actions including arguments, amendment of claims, additional materials if provided.
    - All forms submitted to the USPTO e.g. Oath and Declaration, Bibliographic Data sheet, fee worksheet, Extension of time for Office Action response, power of attorney, change of address, issue fee payment etc..

Figures 8.1 and 8.2 show an example of prosecution history available in public PAIR. Specific contents available in public PAIR depend on the patent and the type of transactions that occurred during the patent prosecution. The perspective licensees/buyers or litigators are often looking for peculiarities in prosecution history that may damper the strength of the patent. Examples of those peculiarities include:

1. Any arguments the applicant has made in order to overcome rejections such as explanation of claim languages that may have inevitably narrowed the scope of the claim.

Mail Room Date ⇅	Document Code ⇅	Document Description ⇅
06-22-2005	TRNA	Transmittal of New Application
06-22-2005	136A	Authorization for Extension of Time all replies
06-22-2005	SPEC	Specification
06-22-2005	CLM	Claims
06-22-2005	ABST	Abstract
06-22-2005	DRW	Drawings-only black and white line drawings
06-22-2005	OATH	Oath or Declaration filed
06-22-2005	WFEE	Fee Worksheet (PTO-06)
06-22-2005	WFEE	Fee Worksheet (PTO-06)
06-22-2005	ADS	Application Data Sheet
06-22-2005	IDS	Information Disclosure Statement (IDS) Filed (SB/08)
06-22-2005	NPL	NPL Documents
06-22-2005	NPL	NPL Documents
10-17-2006	SRNT	Examiner's search strategy and results
10-27-2006	CTNF	Non-Final Rejection
10-27-2006	1449	List of References cited by applicant and considered by examiner
10-27-2006	892	List of references cited by examiner
10-27-2006	FWCLM	Index of Claims
10-27-2006	BIB	Bibliographic Data Sheet
10-27-2006	SRFW	Search information including classification, databases and other

Fig. 8.1 A snapshot of prosecution history in public PAIR.

2. Any amendment of claims. The amendment of claims is usually accomplished by adding additional limiting languages in the claim. Such additional limiting languages usually exhibit the weakness of the invention in the presence of prior art.

3. Any actions that are not based on technical merits to overcome any rejections. Examples include any terminal disclaimer, swear-back of priority dates, correction of inventorship etc.

07-16-2007	REM	Applicant Arguments/Remarks Made in an Amendment
07-16-2007	DIST	Terminal Disclaimer Filed
07-16-2007	N417	EFS Acknowledgment Receipt
07-16-2007	WFEE	Fee Worksheet (PTO-06)
07-16-2007	WFEE	Fee Worksheet (PTO-06)
07-19-2007	SRNT	Examiner's search strategy and results
07-23-2007	DISQ	Terminal Disclaimer Approval form used within the USPTO
07-26-2007	NOA	Notice of Allowance and Fees Due (PTOL-85)
07-26-2007	NOA	Notice of Allowance and Fees Due (PTOL-85)
07-26-2007	BIB	Bibliographic Data Sheet
07-26-2007	IIFW	Issue Information including classification, examiner, name, claim, renumbering, etc.
07-26-2007	FWCLM	Index of Claims
07-26-2007	SRFW	Search information including classification, databases and other search related notes
09-25-2007	IFEE	Issue Fee Payment (PTO-85B)
09-25-2007	WFEE	Fee Worksheet (PTO-06)
09-25-2007	N417	EFS Acknowledgment Receipt
10-10-2007	ISSUE.NTF	Issue Notification
12-19-2007	COCIN	Request for Certificate of Correction
12-19-2007	N417	EFS Acknowledgment Receipt
04-15-2008	COCOUT	Certificate of Correction - Post Issue Communication

Fig. 8.2 A snapshot of prosecution history in public PAIR (continued).

It is therefore extremely important to maintain a clean history during the prosecution. A clean prosecution history means fewer or no red flags that may be raised later. You would need to think twice before you submit any response to Office Actions as anything you submit will become a permanent record in the prosecution history and may adversely affect the use, sales or enforcement of your patent.

A common mistake during patent prosecution is to rush amending claims in every Office Action in order to get around the prior art cited by the examiner. If you are confident on the technical merit of your invention in the presence of prior art, a quick suggestion would be to stick to your ground and present arguments rather than amending your claims. Patent prosecution, especially responding to Office rejections, can be complex and requires tactics. This will be covered in Chapter 9.

8.2   Response to Office Action

This book encourages inventors to get involved in responding to every single Office Action that is based on technical merits. If you are not invited, request such opportunity directly from the attorney firm you are working with.

There are several key areas you should contribute to the preparation of Office Action response:

1. If you believe that the arguments made by the examiner in rejecting the claims are inappropriate, remarks or arguments should be made to address these issues. You want to make sure the remarks are right on the point and addressing examiner's arguments. If you read an Office Action rejection, you will notice that the examiner usually lists his/her arguments clearly one by one corresponding to each element of your claim. Your remarks in the rebuttal should also be one on one corresponding to examiner's argument. In case the examiner's arguments were not addressed or addressed but not persuasive, a second or final rejection is likely to be made by the examiner.
2. Amendments to claims. There are two things an inventor should act as a gate keeper:
    • Make sure the attorney is not rushing to amend claims in order to get around the prior art cited by the examiner. Sometimes, the cited prior art has little to do with the subject matter in the application. In this case, counter-arguments should be presented instead of rushing to resolve the case.

- If the prior art does appear to be relevant and material to the pending claims, and an amendment of claim is needed, you should make sure that the added limiting language in the claim does not drastically limit the scope of the invention. Remember that every record in the prosecution will go to the prosecution history, which will be open to public for inspection.

3. Deadlines. There is a six months statutory requirement to file a response to the Office Action. However, ordinarily, a shortened deadline of only three months is given (or sometimes shorter depending on the issue) and any extension beyond three months would incur an extension fee. It will be to your best interest to make sure that the attorney responses in a timely manner not only to save money on extension fees, but also to help advance the patent case diligently. An early issuance of a patent is the ultimate interest of both inventors and patent owners.

8.3   Duty of Disclosure

The duty of filing information disclosure statement (IDS) should be continuously carried out until either issue fees are paid (if claims are allowed), application is withdrawn or canceled. This duty also applies to individuals in addition to inventors themselves. Those who are involved in the preparation and prosecution of the patent application, such as patent attorney or agent, should all have the duty to disclose. On the other hand, an individual assignee having business interest in the patent may not be obliged to comply with the duty of disclosure if he or she is not involved in the preparation or prosecution of the application.

What needs to be disclosed? Basically any information (whether new issued patents, applications, academic papers, product literatures etc.) that you uncover between filing and when your claims are allowed and that you think material to your claims should be disclosed to the USPTO.

When do you need to disclose? File the information disclosure statement (IDS) together with your patent application or separately within three months from discovering the information. Furthermore, the

IDS only needs to be filed for nonprovisional applications and does not apply to provisional applications.

8.4   Restriction and Election Requirements

8.4.1   *What is Restriction Requirement?*

As the patent rule states, if two or more independent and distinct inventions are claimed in a single application, the examiner will require the applicant to elect one invention, to which the claims will be restricted[1].

The restriction requirement will usually be made by the examiner if, from the view of the examiner, there are two inventions claimed in the application that can be decoupled without one affecting the other. In one scenario, one invention is a process and the other invention is a product made by the process. If it can be shown that the process is not an obvious process of making the product and the process can be used to make different products, or the product can be made by another and materially different process, the two inventions are distinct and restriction requirement will be made.

In one example, if the same invention describes a table with a decorative edge on the surface of the table and a routing technique of making such decorative edge, the invention of the table and routing technique are distinct and should be separated. This is because the routing technique of making decorative edge can also be used to make decorative edges for other furniture or surfaces. Similarly, the decorative edge of a table may be made by employing other routing techniques.

In another example, an invention discloses an image compression technique that treats image as graphics and text separately as the first invention; and a segmentation technique that separates graphics and text for an image as the second invention. Because the segmentation technique separates graphics and text from an image, such separation can be used for other purposes like display or transmission of an image.

---

[1] 37 CFR 1.142.

Further, the separation of graphics and text from an image can be done by an alternative scheme. Therefore, the two inventions are distinct and should be restricted.

In the same example, if the image compression requires the segmentation process to be specifically tuned and render it with no other use, the two inventions are not distinct.

8.4.2   *What Options Do You Have After Receiving Restriction Requirement?*

Although in most circumstances an applicant would concur with the examiner's restriction requirement by electing one invention, you do have the option to pursue otherwise and petition for reconsideration of such requirement if you do not agree with the examiner's decision.

Figure 8.3 shows two options available to you when you agree or not agree with examiner's restriction requirement, respectively. For both options, you MUST reply with your election of one group even if you intend to file petition for reconsideration. This is because the examiner wants to maintain his option what group to choose should he later deny your petition and make the restriction requirement final. Having known your election in advance helps to expedite the process by avoiding another Office Action.

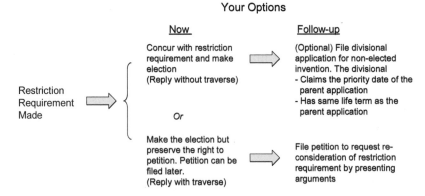

Fig. 8.3 Restriction requirement and applicant's options.

If you concur with the examiner's decision, you should examine the two groups (or multiple groups) of claims corresponding to each invention and choose the most important one. In a follow up action, you shall also make your judgment whether it is worth pursuing the nonelected invention in a divisional application. If it is, file your divisional application to cover the nonelected invention while the parent patent application is still pending. The divisional application is a special case of continuation application and claims the benefit of the priority date of the parent application yet it also has a shortened life – it expires the same time as the parent patent.

If you do not agree with the examiner's restriction requirement, a follow up action of your reply is to file a petition to request reconsideration of such requirement by presenting your arguments why the two (or more) inventions are not separable.

8.5   Overcoming Rejections

Do not be easily discouraged when your first Office Action or even the second one rejects all of your claims. It is quite common. We will devote our attention to this topic in Chapter 9.

8.6   When Conditional Allowance is Received

There are times when all independent claims are rejected but some dependent claims allowed. As we have discussed in Chapter 4, a dependent claim includes all limitations in its preceding independent claim. Therefore, a dependent claim being allowed does not mean such dependent claim alone is allowable.

In order for the allowed dependent claim to sustain, all limitations in its preceding independent claim have to be incorporated. Therefore, an attorney may likely amend the claim as suggested in Fig. 8.4, in a pseudo claim language.

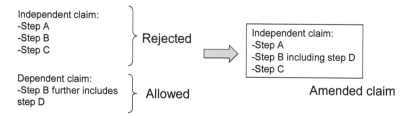

Fig. 8.4 Amendment of claim.

The responsibility in dealing with conditional allowance lies on the inventor and considerations should be taken into account from both technical and business perspectives as the following:

1. Does the rejection have any ground on technical merits? How similar are the pending claims to the prior art cited by the examiner?
2. If you concur with the examiner's rejection, do you want to continue with the amended claim? Is the amended claim still giving you sufficient protection? In the example shown in Fig. 8.4, one question you need to ask is whether the combination of steps as suggested by the amended claim is still practical and if people can get around the combination easily?

At this point, you are glad your claims will be at least allowed. On the other hand, you would want to clarify what exclusive rights you are going to receive with such conditional allowance and make sure it still has commercial and market potential.

8.7   Telephone Interview with the Examiner

If it appears that possible misunderstandings exist during patent prosecution and your arguments may not be as persuasive to the examiner, it is worthwhile considering requesting a phone interview with the examiner who is handling the case. Although an interview is sometimes conducted after the first Office Action, it is often more productive to request it after the second or final Office Action, if at which time there are still substantial issues and differences between the examiner and the applicant.

8.7.1 How Should an Inventor Get Involved in a Telephone Interview with the Examiner?

In reality, an inventor rarely participates in the telephone interview. The main reason is that discussions in this occasion may involve issues of law that may not be apparent to an inventor who is passionate about defending the merits of his invention. Such passion may sometimes cause the inventor to make innocent misstatements that may have debilitating legal implications, which can be distractive to the attorney who is conducting the interview such that he has to worry about rescuing the inventor's misstatements. You must trust your attorney or agent to conduct the interview with the examiner.

8.7.2 How Can an Inventor Contribute to the Preparation of the Interview?

An interview usually runs only about 30 minutes; therefore, it is important that the attorney who is conducting the interview with the examiner is well prepared. He needs to present all the arguments in an organized way to make them relevant to the issues, and achieve the ultimate goal of reaching an agreement with the examiner.

Such interview cannot be conducted well without the help of the inventor. An inventor should be actively consulted by the attorney in order to prepare such interview. As an inventor, you can make the following key contributions:

1. To educate your attorney/agent and familiarize him with the case by providing enough technical background.
2. A proposal listing issues raised in the Office Action and corresponding sensible arguments is always helpful for the attorney to prepare for the interview. The attorney's statements have to be limited to 15 to 20 minutes in the 30 minutes time slot allowed. Therefore, the arguments in the proposal need to be simple, straightforward and on the point. From technical point of view, you

may have, for example, five arguments to support your rebuttal on the same issue raised by the examiner. List them in the order of importance so the attorney can make sure to present key arguments without losing focus and relevancy to the issue.

8.8   When Final Rejection is Received

Do not panic when you receive a final Office Action rejecting all your claims. The word "final" does not mean the end of the patent prosecution although the arguments that may be presented by the applicants are limited.

If all claims are rejected, you need to decide to either continue arguing or abandon your case. It is not uncommon for a patent application to get a final Office Action with all claims rejected. Your attorney will advise you of your options.

Naturally, your attorney may attempt to schedule an interview with the examiner, which process was explained in the preceding section. The key to success is to present a fairly simple proposal that concisely addresses the remaining issues raised in Office Actions. There were precedents that a patent was allowed after a final rejection had been made.

Traditionally, if the interview with the examiner is unfeasible or unsuccessful, the next step is to file an appeal with the Board of Patent Appeals and Interferences (BPAI), who is still under the administration of the USPTO but above the level of patent examiner. This process, however, is a lengthy procedure that can be costly.

Alternatively, people commonly let the case close and file a continuation application, particularly, request for continued examination (RCE) to re-open the case[2]. The option of RCE gives applicant another opportunity for a second complete examination, during which a new approach may be taken in addressing any remaining issues raised by the examiner before.

---

[2] The RCE must be filed before the statutory deadline for the earlier (parent) case, i.e. six months from the final rejection.

8.9   Appeal

Appeal is a more formal procedure to bring the issue up to the Board of Patent Appeals and Interferences in the USPTO after final rejection is made. An appeal will be normally heard by three Board members. One of the technical requirements is that the applicant must file an appeal brief to support his/her position. Optionally, an oral hearing can also be requested.

The current fee on filing an appeal is US$500. In addition, the fee for filing an appeal brief in support of the appeal is US$500 and requesting an oral hearing is US$1000. The total cost can add up quickly considering attorney fees for preparing the appeal brief and attending the oral hearing if so requested.

The critical piece of work for appeal is the appeal brief, in which the inventor and attorney must present key arguments to address the issues raised in the examiner's Office Action in an organized way such that they are simple, concise, easy to comprehend and right to the point. It is not always feasible and efficient to list all the arguments you have. Rather, you should limit the issues and decide on the key and crucial arguments you want to present in the appeal brief. The rule of thumb is: having more than three issues in a brief suggests that you do not have a strong appeal.

8.10   When Your Claims are Allowed at the First Office Action

An extreme situation in patent prosecution is that you may get all your independent claims allowed at the first Office Action. Should you be happy about it?

If such scenario occurs, it is either because your invention is possibly something so innovative that no one has ever invented anything remotely related to it, or because your claims are unnecessarily too narrow. The chance is likely to be the latter. You believe you have done a good job at patent filing and have attempted to draft the broadest claim you can. However, it does not hurt to take another critical look at your claim and see whether it is unnecessarily too narrow.

Even if you have received Notice of Allowance it is not too late to amend your claims and broaden them as needed, as long as you have not paid issue fees. If allowed claims should be broadened and you believe can be broadened, discuss with your attorney on your options and determine the best approach.

8.11 Protest

During your patent pending period, you may receive a protest submitted by a third party. Any member of the public can submit a protest against a pending application. A protest serves the purpose of bringing information to the attention of the USPTO while the application in question is still pending. A protest in accordance with the rule will be considered by the examiner.

The protest rule to be in compliance by a third party primarily includes:

1. A protest must be submitted within two months of the publication of the patent application or the mailing of a notice of allowance, whichever comes first.
2. A protest must include a list of patents, publications or other information (trade show brochures, website links etc.) relied upon.
3. A protest must include a copy of each item provided and concise explanation of the relevance of each item.

By law, unless the examiner requests the applicant to file comments on the protest or reply to the protest and answer any specific questions raised by the protest, the applicant has no duty or does not need to reply to the protest. However, it will be beneficial for the attorney and inventor to review those materials provided by the protester to make sure they are not material to their pending application. By doing so, they can be confident that any effort going forward is still worthwhile.

Website links can be brought by the protestor. To examine the website link submitted in the protest, a good tool is the wayback machine[3], which archives millions of web pages that go back to several years. It gives you a good information about what was available at certain times in the past prior to your priority date.

Note that once the protest is submitted, the protester's participation ends. The protester will not be informed as to the status of the application or any Office Actions.

8.12 Continuation-in-Part (CIP) and Chain of Co-pending Applications

Continuation-in-Part (CIP) is different from other continuation application (e.g. RCE) mentioned earlier that CIP allows inventors to introduce new matters. The same subject matter in CIP that has also been disclosed in the preceding application (parent application) claims the benefit of original priority date, whereas claims relating to any new matters introduced in the continuation application are entitled to the priority date as the date of CIP filing.

From technical perspective, it is often proper to file CIP if the new invention largely depends on what disclosed in the parent application plus some incremental improvements.

From legal perspective, CIP brings the benefits of continuity and simpler filing as opposed to filing a separate application. The filing of CIP can prevent the USPTO from citing information disclosed in the parent case as an obstacle that blocks the inventor's own second application. Because of the continuity between CIP and its parent application for the common subject matters that have been disclosed in both applications, it is often practical to file CIP and abandon the parent application, whereas the original priority filing date is still carried over. Note, CIP must be filed while the parent application is still pending in order to maintain the continuity.

The advantage of CIP is that an applicant buys extra time and still be able to amend claims relating to the subject matters described in the parent application. For this reason, many strategic applicants (e.g.

---

[3] http://www.archive.org.

corporations) want to continue filing CIP as a chain of co-pending applications while they continue making improvements to their products. The so-called chain of co-pending applications means filing a CIP while the parent application is still pending, and filing another CIP while the first CIP is still pending, so on and so forth. The benefit for doing this is that you can monitor how the market evolves during the series of CIP's and amend claims relating to the first parent application to better reflect the market use. Therefore, you can better catch infringers.

The downside of CIP is the shortened life of the continuation patent. For common subject matters CIP's life term is the same as the original application.

Chapter 9

Tactics For Overcoming Rejections

Overcoming rejections from Office Action and filing correspondences are a major part of the prosecution. These actions involve both inventors with in-depth knowledge of technology and attorneys who are familiar with laws and rules. Only when these people work together can the best strategy be developed for overcoming any rejections.

A common pitfall in dealing with Office Action rejections, partially due to the lack of participation from inventors, is the rush of amending claims that can adversely affect the scope of the claims as originally intended. Amending claims is not a simple legal matter; it is also a business decision since claims relate to the scope of final exclusive rights and economic value they will result into. This business decision should naturally be derived from the expertise of inventors who have much insight in both technology as well as existing and potential market.

This chapter is a continuation of Chapter 8 and gives detailed discussions on the basis of several common Office Action rejections, and tactics how you shall overcome them. When you finish reading this chapter, you will be comfortable with reading Office Actions from the USPTO examiners and understanding the issues they raise, discussing the rebuttal strategy more comprehensively with your attorney and providing insightful opinions to the case.

9.1 Common Rejections on the Merits

Among rejections on the merits the following are commonly seen: 35 USC 112 (112), 35 USC 102 (102) and 35 USC 103 (103).

112 First Paragraph Rejection – The first paragraph of 35 USC 112 is very often cited in the rejection to raise issues that relate to the written description requirement such as enablement, new matter and best mode. Subsequent paragraphs in 35 USC 112 may be cited in the rejection to raise issues in claim structure and indefiniteness, which can often be corrected by the attorney.

102 Rejection – The 102 rejection concerns with novelty requirement. Claims may be rejected because they are anticipated by a prior art. By anticipation, it means that each and every element set forth in the claim in the pending application is found expressly or inherently in the prior art reference.

103 Rejection – The 103 rejection concerns nonobviousness requirement. This requirement maintains that if it would have been obvious to anyone ordinarily skilled in the art, at the time an invention was made, to produce the invention in the manner disclosed, the invention is not patentable. The obviousness rejection is usually made in view of the teaching of one or multiple prior art references. In case of multiple prior arts used in rejecting a claim, the examiner is likely to make the argument that it is obvious to combine the teachings of these multiple references to produce the claimed invention. The burden then shifts to the inventor to prove his or her invention is not obvious in light of the combination of prior arts.

Different types of rejections require different strategies. The remainder of this chapter gives you insights on how these rejections should be handled.

9.2   112 First Paragraph Rejection

9.2.1   *Enablement*

The 112 first paragraph rejection relates to how-to-use aspect of the enablement requirement, and requires claims to indicate how the use of the invention can be carried out, or how the invention can be used. The 112 first paragraph rejection is sometimes associated with the utility requirement of 101 [1] not being met, i.e. claims are nonuseful or inoperative. If claims are not useful, it automatically fails the 112 requirement, i.e. it fails to show how the invention can be used.

In most cases though, the 112 paragraph rejection is made when utility requirement of 101 is met. A number of situations may result in a 112 first paragraph rejection:

1. A critical feature which is taught as critical in the specification is not cited in the claims. The critical feature would be considered limitation in the claims, and omission of this limitation can raise the issue whether the inventor is entitled to a broader, more generic invention.
2. New matters are considered to have been introduced. Relating to 112 first paragraph rejection, new matters that have been introduced to the claims cannot find their support in the specification therefore new claims cannot be enabled.
3. Any other changes made to the claims may raise the issue whether one skilled in the art would consider the changes to be inherently supported by the original specification.

As can be seen, both broadening a claim   (i.e. omitting critical features) and narrowing a claim (by adding something new) may trigger 112 first paragraph rejection. To rebut this rejection based on technical merits, there are two directions that you may direct your effort to:

1. If it is the critical feature taught in the specification but not cited in the claims, you would need to provide justification whether the

---

[1] 35 USC 101.

critical feature is indeed critical and whether it should be included in the claims. Be aware not to easily follow the examiner's suggestions and amend your claims. For example, you are teaching a handheld device for controlling all home devices using infrared and in your claim you only mention wireless as the communication link. If your claims are rejected due to enablement, the argument lies upon whether the infrared is a critical feature, or only an exemplary protocol of the wireless communication. It depends on how your teaching in light of infrared can be applicable or inherited to other wireless means according to one skilled in the art.

2. If the rejection is about new matters introduced in the claim, check whether it is inherently supported elsewhere in the specification, drawings, abstract etc. before you give it up by canceling the "new matter".

9.2.2   New Matter

Regarding new matter issue it is important for the inventor to examine the issue himself and determine whether it is truly new matter. The following may give some hints on what is not new matter:

1. Information contained in any of the abstract, specification, drawings or claims may be added to any of the other part in this group without introducing new matter.
2. The claim is part of the specification. If an application as originally filed contains a claim disclosing material not disclosed in the remainder of the specification, the inventor may amend the specification to include the claimed subject matter.
3. A subject matter does not have to be explicitly said in the original specification, yet can be considered as being disclosed. As described in MPEP[2], a patent application disclosing a device that inherently performs a function is considered as disclosing that function although it says nothing explicitly concerning it. Therefore, an application may later be amended to recite the function without introducing new matter.

---

[2] MPEP 2163.07 (a).

9.2.3   *Best Mode*

Best mode is also part of 112 first paragraph[3], and it has already been mentioned in a few places in previous chapters. Best mode is not commonly a cause of rejection during patent prosecution. However, it is an important requirement by law and has been the topic in many litigation cases. Among those litigations, the common decision made at the court was whether the inventor possessed a best mode for practicing the invention at the time of filing, and if so, whether the written description disclosed the best mode such that one ordinarily skilled in the art could practice it.

For the above reasons, best mode is usually not being challenged in patent prosecution. It is only worth the effort if a patent is being involved in a litigation case and an invalidation attempt of the patent shall be made.

9.3   102 Rejection and Prior Art

Once a 102 rejection is received, you would need to first determine whether the reference cited in the examiner's rejection has been used properly. This section gives detailed illustrations of the basis of 102 rejection and teaches you tactics on how to overcome 102 rejection.

9.3.1   *Anatomy of 102*

The basis of 102 rejection is included in various sections of Patent Law 35 USC 102. Table 9.1 summarizes most commonly seen 102 criteria that may qualify a prior art.

As illustrated, a prior art on which 102 is based is mainly being looked at by: type of reference, country, who and when.

---

[3] In 35 U.S.C. 112, "The specification shall contain a written description of the invention, and of the manner and process of making and using it, in such full, clear, concise, and exact terms as to enable any person skilled in the art to which it pertains, or with which it is most nearly connected, to make and use the same, and shall set forth the best mode contemplated by the inventor of carrying out his invention."

Table 9.1 Criteria qualifying prior art in 102.

	Types of Reference	Country	By Who	When (relative to the patent app priority date)
102(a)	Public used or known	This	By others	Occurred before
	Patented or printed publication (inc. patent or published patent app)	This/foreign		
102(b)	*Printed publication	This/foreign	Self/other	Published 12 mos. before
	*Public use or public/private sale	This		
102 (c)	*Invention has been abandoned.			
102(d)	*Inventor's certificate filed		Same or legal representatives, same invention	12 mos. before
	*Patent granted or certificate issued (no need to publish)	Foreign		Before
102(e)	Patent application publication	This	By another	Filed before
	Or patent granted			Filed before
	Or (a) International app filed on or after 11/29/00 and PCT pub in English	This/foreign	By another	Filed Int. App (IA) before
	Or (b) International app entering National stage (fee, English, declaration)	This		Filed Int. App. (IA) before

* statutory bar

Types of 102 References

The types of references used in 102 rejections include:

1. Public use (such as demonstration).
2. Private or public sale (of product made from the invention, regardless whether you have made profit or not).
3. Publications (including granted patents or published patent application).
4. Printed publications (such as journal article, library copies etc.)
5. Granted patents or applications having obtained certificate of rights (applicable to European patent).
6. International patent applications (PCT).

For printed publication, the presence of a single copy thesis in a university library has been held in the court to constitute publication as the copy of the thesis being made available at the library indicates that it can be accessed publicly with the aid of library catalog regardless whether the library catalog is on-line or not.

Country of References

Note that references cited for 102 rejections are not limited to this country. As shown in Table 9.1, the following foreign references may be used as a prior art in 102 rejection:

1. 102(a): patent or printed patent application in any country.
2. 102(b): printed publication (e.g. magazine, journal article) in any country.
3. 102(d):
   a. a patent application filed by the same applicant/legal representative in a foreign country.
   b. a European patent granted or obtained certificate of rights.
4. 102(e): PCT application filed on or after 11/29/2000 and published in English.

References eligible from foreign sources are patents, patent application publications, printed publications; whereas the public use or public/private sale is only limited to the U.S. For example, you may have already sold your products (based on your invention) in a foreign country. Later, you can still file a patent application in the U.S.

Authors of References

The author of reference can either be inventor (under examination) himself or others depending on the types of references. For example, 102(b) and 102(d) can be both applicable to inventor himself. In other words, your early patent or application can be a bar to your own invention. Note that "Others" refers to any entity which is different from the inventive entity (inventor). The entity needs to differ only by one person to be considered as "others".

Date of References

The eligibility of prior art is largely based on its reference date relative to the priority date of the application under examination. For example, under 102(a), if the same inventive matter by others is known in public in this country before your priority date, it may become a prior art to bar your application. Also under 102(a), if the same inventive matter has been published by others in this or foreign country before your priority date, it may bar your application.

9.3.2   *Statutory Requirement and "Swear Back" of Date*

Statutory requirement applies to 102(b), (c), (d), in which one may not patent an invention if he has already abandoned previously; or if the prior art has already been made public (e.g. published) more than 12 months prior to the filing date of the pending application. For 102(c), the abandonment may be due to explicit abandonment from the applicant or other actions such as failure to respond to Office Actions.

If your claim is rejected based on nonstatutory requirement, i.e. any of 102(a) or (e), you should first look at the possibility of "swear back" of date to disqualify cited prior art used in the rejection. "Swear back" is a very effective tool in eliminating some prior art based on which you claims are rejected. If you can provide adequate evidence that your invention was conceived before the effective filing date of the prior art, you may disqualify such prior art.

We have discussed before about keeping record and evidence of your invention, which can prove the date of the conception of your invention and can be used to move your priority date early. Between 102(a) and 102(e), using "swear back" to overcome 102(e) may be more difficult since 102(e) affords earlier effective date because it uses the filing date of the reference in comparison to the publication date.

If your claim is rejected based on the statutory requirement or statutory bar, i.e. any of 102(b), (c) and (d), you cannot "swear back" of your priority date. Instead, you must focus on comparing the merits of your invention with the reference in your argument, which will be discussed in the next section.

9.3.3 *Examples of Prior Art and Statutory Date*

Example 1: Prior Art

Question: You conceived a new process and, few months later, in September 2000 you filed a patent application. Assuming that you were not aware of any of the following facts at the time of your conception, which of the following facts will NOT bar your application from obtaining a U.S. patent?

a) A written disclosure of the process in a printed publication which was published in France in December 1999;

b) A written disclosure of the process by another author in a printed publication which was published in the U.S. in October 1999;

c) Uses of the process by two oil companies in their manufacturing operations in the U.S. before January 2000; none of the companies regard the process as being considered a proprietary secret.

d) A German scientist made an oral disclosure of the process in December 1999 to the research managers of two German companies.

e) A French scientist made an oral disclosure of the process to all attendees at a seminar in the U.S. in December 1999.

In the above example the correct answer is d. The presentation made by the German scientist is not considered public thus it does not belong to any reference listed in 102 criteria. All other answers would be 102(a) references and would be a bar from you obtaining a U.S. patent. Because of 102(a), all other answers would not be a statutory bar and can be "swore back" if adequate evidence can be provided.

Example 2: Statutory Requirement

You invented a new device on May 10, 2005, then you secretly went to California and sold four of your devices to a Canadian company. On July 5, 2005, the Canadian company started using your device in Canada and after six months or so experimentation the company has widely publicized in Canada and the U.S. information about your device. On June 1, 2006, you tried to decide what your option is and whether you can file a patent on your new device, at least to protect your interests in the U.S. market. Which of the following is correct?

a) You are barred from obtaining a U.S. patent on your device because it was sold more than one year before June 1, 2006.

b) You are not barred from obtaining a U.S. patent on your device because you sold to a foreign company, not a U.S. company.

c) You are not barred from obtaining a U.S. patent on your device because your sale to the Canadian company was not a public sale.

d) You are not barred from obtaining a U.S. patent on your device because it was used by the Canadian company only in Canada and not in the U.S.

Answer a is correct. The reference prior art is the private sale that occurred in U.S. (this country) on May 10, 2005, which is more than 12 months before your intended filing date of June 1, 2006. This falls into 102(b) rejection and it is a statutory bar that cannot be "swore back".

One exception to the "use or sale" in 102(b) is that the "use or sale" is experimental and there was some necessity for public testing and the experiment was under the supervision and control of the inventor. In such constrained environment, developmental testing is permitted, and there is no bar under 102(b).

Example 3: Swear Back

Here is an excerpted prosecution history of the patent serial number 08/727,820. Figure 9.1 shows the rejection by the examiner on all independent claims under 102(a) as anticipated (taught) by Meeker. The applicant took the combined approach of both amending claims and arguing that their claims are distinguishable from the prior art cited. But they failed to persuade the examiner. The rejections were made final. The applicant filed continuation application to resume the examination and used similar approach to overcome the rejection and failed again. A final rejection was made again in the continuation application and a second continuation application was filed. The claims were rejected again in the second continuation application as anticipated by Meeker as before.

---

8.   Claim 1 is rejected under 35 U.S.C. 102(a) as being anticipated by Meeker,

"AnimNav.java Version 1.0.0", http://www.realtime.net/~elijah/old/jindex.htm, 1/4/96, pp. 1-

14 (hereinafter Meeker).

Fig. 9.1 Illustration of 102 rejection.

III. Claim Rejections Under 35 U.S.C. § 102 and § 103:

Applicants first note that the effective date given to the Meeker reference is not a

publication date. The date noted by the Examiner (1/4/96) is merely a date included in

the code as a creation date. The Examiner has not provided evidence of a publication

date for this reference. However, regardless of the actual publication date of the Meeker

reference, applicants' invention was reduced to practice prior to the January 4, 1996 date,

therefore, the Meeker reference is not a prior art reference and the rejection should be

removed.

Attached hereto is a Declaration by the inventors that establishes completion of

the invention in this application at a date prior to January 4, 1996. The Declaration

includes an Exhibit showing code that was created prior to January 4, 1996. As described

in the Declaration, the code performs the claimed invention.

Accordingly, claims 1-19 are submitted as patentable over the references cited by

the Examiner.

Fig. 9.2 Overcoming 102 rejection via "swear back".

Finally, the applicant took a different approach by "swearing back" of their date in order to overcome the rejection. The arguments are shown in Fig. 9.2.

Basically, the inventors filed declaration attaching a piece of source code and declared that the code was created prior to January 4, 1996, the alleged publication date of the reference cited by the examiner. The declaration and source code did not show the particular date of creation of the source code, but rather the applicant stated the source code was created prior to the January 4, 1996 date to indicate the invention was conceived before this date as well. This "swear back" through inventors' declaration on the date of source code succeeded and claims were allowed.

In this case, the "swear back" approach was indeed very effective and "clean" without having to amend claims. In fact, this approach could have been taken much earlier to avoid two unnecessary continuation applications.

9.4   Overcoming 102 Rejection

The essential part of 102 is the novelty requirement based on technical merits of the invention, in which every element of the claim is anticipated by the prior art reference. The anticipation means "found", "taught", "expressly or inherently described".

9.4.1   Common Approaches

The 102 rejection based on (a), (b) and (e) are common in Office Actions and the ways to overcome 102 rejection are outlined in the MPEP[4] and elaborated further in detail as below.

1. Persuasively argue that the claims are patentably distinguishable from the prior art.
2. Amend the claims to patentably distinguish over the prior art.

---

[4] MPEP 706.02(b).

3. Perfect the priority date in several possible ways so the prior art reference is not antedate your priority date:
   a. "Swear back" of your priority date if the rejection is not based on statutory bar. This has been illustrated extensively in the previous section and is often an effective approach.
   b. If you have filed your patents previously either domestic or foreign, you may want to "link" to your prior invention so your pending application may claim the benefit of prior invention filing date. The condition is that other requirements (e.g. 12-month grace period, enablement and description requirements etc.) are also met.
4. If the rejection is based on another of your own invention but treated as "another", you may file an affidavit or declaration showing that the reference invention is your own work and not by "another". This rejection occurs mostly when there is a common assignee or common but nonidentical list of inventors between your application and the prior art reference.

Among these common approaches, No. 3 and No. 4 should be attempted first because if you are able to pursue, your arguments will be objective and should be concurred by the examiner. The approaches No. 1 and No. 2 are less preferable to No. 3 and No. 4 because any arguments or changes you make will all undergo examiner's subjective review and have a chance of being rejected again. The subject matter of No. 1 will be further taken up in the remainder of this section.

9.4.2   *Distinguishing Claims*

Many times your choice is either arguing that your claims are distinguishable from the prior art or amending your claims so they become distinguishable over the prior art. These two efforts have some commonalities: they all require you to be skillful in distinguishing your claims from the prior art.

To be clear, arguing 102 rejection based on the merit requires comparison between your claims and prior arts vis-à-vis each element of your claims and arguments used by the examiner in rejecting them. The following guideline can help you pursue this:

1. In terms of prior art, what is being considered by the examiner in rejecting your claim is not limited to the claims of the prior art. Anything disclosed in the specification can be used to reject your claim.
2. Effectively distinguishing your claims from prior art requires practices and some knowledge of patent laws to think in the same way the examiner does. Passionately arguing the differences yet missing points relating to the guidelines outlined in patent rule is not going to help overcome the rejection.
3. In order for a prior art to bar your patent from being granted, it has to anticipate every single element in your claim. Therefore, in your argument, you would need to examine closely the prior art cited by the examiner and particularly each argument and citation made by the examiner that corresponds to each element in your claim. As long as you break the rejection on at least one of the elements in your claim, you shall succeed disqualifying the prior art.

Sounds like a simple job, does it not? However, if your argument is something like: "We are doing totally different things!", "We are taking different approaches!", "The prior art describes only a particular implementation whereas my invention has a much broader scope" etc, you need to read on.

As an inventor, the best way to train yourself is to get every opportunity to work with the attorney or agent handling your case, participate in the Office Action response, express your thoughts and ask questions. In your argument, you will need to avoid the following pitfalls that are not going to make your argument workable.

Word by Word Comparison

If you compare word by word between prior art and your invention, and look for the differences in the use of languages, you are heading in the wrong direction. The anticipation of claims does not require that the languages in your claims be mentioned in the prior art, but any implicit or inherent expression will also be considered as anticipation. Therefore, you need to truly grasp the essence of the prior art and put yourself in the shoes of its inventor or any one skilled in the art. You must ask the question to yourself: can this prior art be easily (implicitly or inherently) extended to achieve my invention?

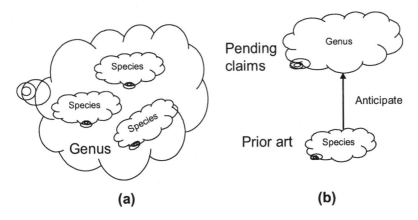

(a)   **(b)**

Fig. 9.3 Genus and species in anticipation of claims.

Species and Genus Situation

A genus may cover many species, and a claim may be made to a genus or a species. As described in MPEP[5], a generic claim cannot be allowed to an applicant if the prior art discloses a species falling within the claimed genus. As illustrated in Fig. 9.3, the species disclosed in the prior art will anticipate the genus claim.

For example, if the pending claim reads as: "... said amplifying circuit containing a device selected from the group consisting of tubes and transistors", and a prior art describes a device made of tubes, the pending claim is anticipated by the prior art. The species and genus situation also occurs mostly in chemical compound patents, and the same guideline can be applied.

---

[5] MPEP 2131.02

If your rejection falls into the species and genus situation, your continuing to argue would perhaps be counter productive. Instead, you may consider amending your claims to exclude species disclosed in the prior art.

Commercial Success or Unexpected Results

According to MPEP[6], evidence of secondary considerations, such as unexpected result or commercial success, is irrelevant to 102 rejections and thus cannot overcome a rejection so based. Unexpected result refers to the showing that the claimed invention generated unexpected results from that of the prior art in order to indicate their substantial difference. This approach can be supplementary in overcoming 103 rejection, but is irrelevant to 102 rejection.

Nonanalogous Art or "Teaches Away"

When rebutting a rejection in the presence of prior art, many inventors intend to argue that the prior art is a totally different thing (i.e. nonanalogous art in patent language); or the prior art is "teaching away" from the claimed invention; or the prior art is not recognized as solving the problem solved by the claimed invention. These arguments or alike, as described in MPEP[7], are not "germane" to a rejection under section 102.

There seems to be a misconception among many people that a reference has to be an analogous art or solving the same problem as stated in the claimed invention. This is not correct as has been held by the court. As stated in MPEP, "... the question of whether a reference is analogous art is not relevant to whether that reference anticipates. A reference may be directed to an entirely different problem than the one addressed by the inventor, or may be from an entirely different field of endeavor than that of the claimed invention, yet the reference is still

---

[6] MPEP 2131.04

[7] MPEP 2131.05.

anticipatory if it explicitly or inherently discloses every limitation recited in the claims".

This clearly adds much sophistication in your thinking when you attempt to overcome 102 rejection. It would be counter productive if you simply try to argue that the prior art is trying to solve a different problem, as did many inventors. You should put your focus on whether prior art truly explicitly or inherently discloses every limitation in your claims vis-à-vis each argument made by the examiner.

To conclude this section, once you receive 102 rejection, explore the possibility of the following in the order of preference:

1. "Swear back" of your priority date.
2. Move your priority date earlier by claiming the benefit of another of your own patent filed domestically or foreign.
3. Rebut examiner's rejection vis-à-vis each of the statement in association with the 102 rejection.
4. Lastly, amend your claims to get around the prior art.

Finally, make sure both you and your attorney or agent do a thorough job on the rebuttal of 102 rejections since you may have only limited chances. Very often the examiner issues a final rejection at the second Office Action.

9.5   103 Rejection

A rejection based on 103 usually requires the teaching from a reference or a combination of elements or features from a number of references that would have been obvious to one with ordinary skills in the art at the time the invention was made. In this section, we focus on 103(a) rejection for it is the most common rejection, and contributions from inventors in the rebuttal are mostly desired. 103(b) is applicable to biotechnology only and 103(c) is dealing with common ownership issues.

9.5.1   *Difference Between 102 Rejection and 103 Rejection*

The key difference between 102 rejection and 103 rejection is that under 102 rejection the reference must teach every element in the pending claim while under 103 rejection the reference does not. In order for 102 rejection to hold, any features not directly disclosed in the reference must be inherently present in order to anticipate the pending claim. Under 103 rejection, the reference does not need to show all features of the invention. If the reference can be modified, and such modification would have been obvious to one of ordinary skill in the art at the time the invention was made, it still anticipates the pending claim.

Normally, the examiner would seek 102 rejection first. Only after he has exhausted the possibility of making rejections based on 102 (novelty) will he analyze under the USPTO guideline in relation to 103 rejections. Therefore, it generally requires more work for the examiner to make 103 rejection.

9.5.2   *Basis of 103 Rejection*

The 103 rejection requires the examiner to make sure the standard of patentability is applied. Particularly, the USPTO policy is to follow the well-known Graham Factual Inquiries from the court decision made at Graham v. John Deere Co. case (1966, case law 383 U.S. 1) in determining obviousness. The main inquiries and their basic considerations are:

The Scope and Content of the Prior Art

Analogous prior art is an important consideration taken into account by the examiner. As expressed in MPEP[8], a reference used under 103 rejection must be analogous prior art. What this means is that the analogous prior art for the purpose of analyzing the obviousness must either be in the field of your invention, or be reasonably pertinent to the particular problem with which your invention is concerned.

---

[8] MPEP 2141.01(a).

Although 103 rejection is only limited to analogous art (as opposed to 102 rejection), the definition of analogous art is pretty broad as "reasonably pertinent" can be interpreted widely. Therefore, arguing that the prior art reference is a nonanalogous art in most cases would be a tough sale.

Furthermore, the reason or motivation for modifying a reference (in order to inherently make the invention obvious) may often suggest what has been done by your invention, but for a different purpose or to solve a different problem. The obviousness rejection can be made so based, and it is not necessary that the prior art must suggest the combination to achieve the same advantage or result discovered by your invention.

The Level of Ordinary Skill in the Art at Time of the Invention

The references must be reviewed without the benefit of impermissible hindsight vision afforded by the claimed invention. When the decision is being made as whether to reject claims, it is necessary to look back to the time the invention was made, often a few years back, what has been taught in the claimed invention. To determine obviousness in the view of one ordinarily skilled in the art, the one skilled in the art must be presented only with the prior art references and guided by the then-accepted wisdom in the art.

The Differences Between the Claimed Invention and the Prior Art

The reference (or multiple combined) must be considered "as a whole" and must suggest the desirability and thus the obviousness of making the combination. In determining the differences between the prior art reference and the pending claims, the issue under 103 rejection is not whether the differences themselves would have been obvious, but whether the claimed invention as a whole would have been obvious. For this reason, the essence or the "gist" of the invention should not be distilled and so based on analyzing the subject matter "as a whole".

Objective Evidence of Nonobviousness

Reasonable expectation of success is the standard, based on which obviousness is determined. In other words, in order to make 103 rejection, when multiple prior art references are combined, the resultant combination will need to generate expected success as can be from your invention.

9.5.3 *Tactics for Overcoming 103 Rejection*

Ultimately, the objective of this book is to give you enough knowledge and present you tactics and choices in the prosecution process that may help you be creative and proactive when working with attorneys or agents. With this objective, some main considerations to be taken into account in the rebuttal of 103 rejections are briefly discussed in the remainder of this section.

1. Obviousness cannot be predicated on what is not known at the time your invention is made, even if the inheritance of a certain feature is later established. You must put yourself in the shoes of one skilled in the art back to when your invention was filed and make sure there is no hindsight vision or disclosure of your invention based on which the obviousness rejection was made.
2. The mere fact that multiple references can be combined does not render the resultant combination obvious over your pending claims unless the prior art suggests the desirability of the combination. From a different perspective, if the proposed modification or combination of the prior art (in order to show obviousness over your invention) are being modified unsatisfactorily for its intended purpose, or the principle of operation of the prior art being modified, the teachings of references are not sufficient to render your claims obvious. If any of the references used in the combination is teaching away from the combined invention, no obviousness rejection shall be made.
3. To show nonobviousness, you may present evidence showing there was no reasonable expectation of success, i.e. the resultant combination of prior art references will not generate expected success as can be from your invention.

4. Secondary considerations. The other examples of factors that may effectively show "objective evidence of nonobviousness" and will be considered have been provided by the court as:

    a. Commercial success or licensing (which are directly attributed to the claimed invention, rather than bundles with other high profit sales).

    b. Long-felt but unsolved needs, which expressed needs must correlate with the problems solved by the claimed invention.

    c. Failure of others. Prior to the claimed invention, other people attempted to achieve the claimed invention but failed.

    d. Copying by others. The fact of other people copying the claimed invention infers that the invention would not have been obvious.

    e, Skepticism of experts prior to the invention is ever conceived. The skepticism raised by experts would discourage one ordinarily skilled in the art from pursuing the path taken by the inventor. The presence of prior art that "teaches away" supports the nonobviousness of the claimed invention.

    f. The term "secondary" does not refer to the importance of the considerations. "The term instead indicates that these considerations necessarily arise second in time, after the invention has been introduced in the market, in contrast to the other Graham factors which focus upon the time the invention was made".[9] The secondary considerations focus on economic rather than technical issues and are believed to provide objective evidence of how interested industry players perceived the claimed invention[10].

---

[9] Truswal Sys. Corp. vs. Hydro-Air Eng'g, 813 F.2d 1207, 1212, 2 USPQ2d 1034, 1038 (1987 Federal Circuit case law).

[10] Heidelberger Druckmaschinen AG vs. Hantscho Commercial Products, Inc., 21 F.3d 1068, 30 USPQ2d 1377 (1994 Federal Circuit case law).

Finally, some counter productive rebuttal arguments include:

1. Use arguments of counsel in lieu of evidence where evidence is necessary. For this very reason, it would not be a good idea to let your attorney or agent handle the correspondence to Office Action alone whereas you may be able to provide any evidence needed. It is sometimes helpful if such evidence is provided by you or other experts in the field along with an affidavit showing this is their true opinion.
2. Argue that the prior art devices are not physically combinable. The test is what the combined teachings suggest to one ordinarily skilled in the art.
3. Attack references individually while the rejection is based on a combination of references. The exception is the use of "swear back" of date to disqualify at least one of the references.

9.6   Admission of Prior Art by Applicant

One thing worth mentioning is that you should always be careful in handling prior art and be aware what may be considered prior art against your claims. Particularly, you may have already admitted a prior art against you without knowing it. Once prior art is admitted, it may be considered by the examiner to reject your claims during patent prosecution or by a third party attempting to invalidate your invention anytime during the life of your patent.

The following are counted as admitted prior art:

1. If the specification identifies another inventive entity's work as "prior art", it is an admission of prior art.
2. A statement by an applicant during prosecution identifying the work of another as "prior art" is an admission of prior art.
3. In Jepson claim (as discussed in Chapter 4), the subject matter of the preamble is implicitly admitted as the prior art work of another inventive entity.
4. Applicant's labeling of "prior art" in the drawings submitted with his application is an admission of prior art.

5. Examiner's statement of common knowledge in the art. If applicant does not reasonably traverse (object to) the well-known statement during the examination, the examiner's statement will be counted.

The following are NOT counted towards admitted prior art:

1. Published information (e.g. Internet) containing no publication or retrieval date.
2. Listing of references in IDS is not taken as an admission that the reference is prior art against the claims.

Always be careful what you disclose and how you state other people's work. Regardless whether you make such statement in your original specification, claims or correspondence during patent prosecution, it will all be recorded in the prosecution history, which will be made public. Such statement can still be used against you during subsequent licensing or sales of your patent as potential buyers or licensees are always looking for risks that a patent may be invalidated by a prior art.

Chapter 10

Post Patent Granting

Once a patent is issued, many inventors think their relations with patents are over. But the grant of a patent is just the beginning. There are still many technical contributions and duties required of the inventor while a patent is in force. Remember, the ultimate goal of filing a patent is to claim a piece of legal right that you can enforce and create commercial values with. This chapter highlights some activities an inventor may encounter post patent granting.

10.1 Publications

Many researchers like both patenting and publishing their inventions. You have learned from Chapter 8 that you should be prudent with any response to the USPTO Office Action during patent prosecution because all records will be archived in prosecution history and will be made for public access. If you intend to publish any academic paper based on your invention, you should exercise the same caution as your paper will be a public record and can be considered by the court in association with your patent when needed. But you may be wondering how a paper can have an impact on your patent that has already been granted.

10.1.1 *No Mentioning of Product in Publications*

I have seen some academic papers from product companies mentioning their specific products and describing how their products work. The author's intention perhaps was to advertise a company's product through publications, yet the risk is that it gives away too much details about the product. In an exemplary paper, the abstract reads like:

"... We present an end-to-end transport protocol called the Video Retrieval Protocol (VRP) for transporting compressed, stored video over a wide-area ATM network to a remotely connected equipment for real-time playback of the transported video stream. VRP is designed to operate over the ABR and VBR+ services of ATM and is targeted for use by next-generation video retrieval applications. The design of VRP is based on the application of three new techniques called spectral filtering, spectral data segmentation and spectral packetizing. Our experimental results on simulation under various network congestion conditions show that VRP performs better than TCP and UDP in terms of the overall perceptual quality of the displayed video stream. This protocol has also been implemented in our flagship product <u>Champion II series</u> and its sale has doubled in the last quarter".

The paper particularly pointed out that the described proprietary protocol has been implemented in the company's Champion II series product. This public information serves as good evidence of use if someone's patent reads on the protocol described in the paper; consequently, the company's Champion II product can be easily found infringing someone's patent without much reverse engineering efforts. In practice, authors of publications are advised not to mention both their and other companies' product names to avoid any legal issues.

10.1.2 *Consistency Between Patent and Publication*

If you are following the patent-then-publish rule, you need to be consistent when describing the same technology in your patent disclosure and in your academic paper. For the same reason mentioned before, any of the public information including your publication can be used in the court in association with your patent should any challenge on your patent arise. Any contradictory information will be unfavorable to your case and can jeopardize the validity of your patent.

As an example, in the same case law *Research Corporation Technologies v. Microsoft* (2006 case law District of Aizona) as mentioned in Section 3.6.2, back in 2001, RCT sued Microsoft for its patents directed to a "blue noise mask" used in halftoning digital images. The new procedure was disclosed in the patent application as being "visually pleasing" and lacking "low frequency graininess at every level of gray". At the same time the inventors published a paper that reported results of "visually annoying clumps" with graininess. In the paper, the inventors repeatedly downplayed the claimed algorithm in favor of another technique that was inconsistent with the patent. That paper was never submitted to the USPTO.

The court found this seemingly contradictory information material because a "reasonable Patent Examiner clearly would have considered [the contradictory information] important to at least the written description and enablement requirement for patentability". As a result, because of the inventor's post-filing publication disparaging the invention, Arizona District Court Judge Manual Real found that the inventors had intention to mislead and deceive the USPTO when they withheld this highly material information and ruled that RCT's patents were unenforceable.

An interesting fact about RCT's patents is that the patents had previously been asserted against several other high tech companies, each of whom had settled out of court and taken a license.

10.2   Reissue

After a patent is issued, a reissue application may be filed to take up the case again, usually in the following scenarios:

1. For any corrective measures such as correction of inventorship.
2. For expanding the scope of claims or broadening of claims.
3. For narrowing the scope of claims.

Technically, the reissue application is treated the same as if the application was filed as nonreissue except it is taken to the examination much quicker at the USPTO. From the inventor's perspective, the effort is slightly different from when an original application or response to Office Action is being filed. The objective of broadening or narrowing the scope of claims often has to do with business considerations taken into account by its patent owners and it is worth exploring in this section. Once the reissue application is filed, the examination at the USPTO is pretty much the same as nonreissue application in a sense that all elements such as enablement, novelty and obviousness will be looked at. Reissue patent claims the same priority date of the original patent, any new claims still have to be supported in the original specification.

10.2.1 *Broadening of Claims*

Should the patent owner feel that the granted claims are made too narrow, he can file reissue application to broaden the claims. A few things you might want to know as an inventor:

1. Expanding one aspect of the claim and at the same time narrowing another aspect of the claim is considered broadening the claim.
2. Adding a new category of claims (e.g. to add a method claim if there was no method claim originally) is considered broadening the claim.
3. Broadening a claim is only allowed within two years of the original patent issue date unless any intent to broaden the claim is indicated in the reissue application filed within the two year time frame.[1]
4. Any broadening of a claim requires oath and declaration by all of the inventors.
5. In broadening your claims, you shall avoid eliminating any limitations you added during the original prosecution in order to make the claims allowed. This is called recapture. It refers to the attempt to regain claim scope previously surrendered, and recapture is not permitted in broadening claims.

---

[1] Patent Law 35 USC 251.

10.2.2 *Narrowing of Claims*

The rule of narrowing of claims is a little loose in comparison to broadening of claims. For instance, there is no requirement of two years within original patent grant date; inventor's oath and declaration is not needed for narrowing of claims only. The question is: why would someone want to narrow his claims if he already received a broader claim?

Section 4.4.1 shows that the structure of independent and dependent claims combined is made to fit claims as tight as possible to a foreseeable future product. In analogy, the objective of narrowing claims is exactly the same. If you accuse someone of infringing your patent only on broad claims, people will wonder whether that broad claim should be granted in the first place and they will try to find prior art to invalidate it. The purpose of drafting dependent claims or adding narrower claims is to increase the chance of someone infringing both broad and narrow claims. Consequently, the risk of the claims being invalidated will be much lower.

The advantage of filing reissue application is that at the time of the filing, you will have much more information about the market, the current or potential use of your invention than you did when you filed your original application. Accordingly, you can draft a set of claims that will fit much better into any accused product.

As a matter of fact, the reason of narrowing claims is often because the market is moving in the direction of the patent or an infringed product is already found. In this case, the attorney's job will be easier now that she can visualize the infringed product and draft a set of claims to make it a tight fit. The new claims will bring a stronger infringement case.

Finally, for inventors, to contribute to the reissue process, you need to mainly pay attention to the following things:

1. After your patent is granted, stay alert for any products that may be related to your invention or that you have a strong reason to believe are using your invention. Bring these to the attention of your legal department or attorney and they will advise the best approach.

2. In preparing reissue application, make sure the accused product is indeed using your invention before you modify your claims to make it a tight fit.

3. In modifying your claims for reissue, you would want to make sure the limitations you are adding to narrow your claims are still supported in your original patent specification, and the new claims are still meeting the novelty and nonobviousness criteria.

PART 4 Business Perspectives and Beyond

Chapter 11

Patent Protection and Beyond

This chapter and the next few chapters in this book discuss some common strategies carried out by corporate patent holders in commercializing their intellectual property assets. They also highlight some special topics in the commercialization process such as patent evaluation, maintenance, sales, licensing and valuation.

11.1 Patenting Should be Business Driven

If the whole idea of patenting is to file a patent for the sake of patent, or to get a piece of paper from the PTO, or prove your intelligence through the grant of your patent, you should not file patent in the first place. Patenting should be completely business driven.

This is the key difference between research ideas and patent ideas, between publishing a paper and filing a patent. Filing a patent should have a clear business objective and motivation in the first place: that is to create something commercially viable and having economic value. Much effort should be continuously made throughout the life of a patent in order to achieve this business objective. Some of the ongoing efforts include:

1. Using the patented invention in one's existing products.
2. Continuously improving, testing and perfecting the invention in an effort to create a new product.
3. Promoting the invention and diligently seeking parties who may adopt the technology and commercialize it.

4. Diligently watching out for any infringers who may be using the invention with or without realizing it.
5. Selling outright and trading patent for cash should the business direction shift away from the invention.

Among these efforts, some are defensive and some are offensive. A patent or a patent portfolio should be properly positioned in terms of its objective and strategy for implementing it.

11.2 Defense Strategy

An unfavorable scenario that can occur to any product company is the injunction when being sued for patent infringement. The court may decide to order an injunction that requires the company to refrain from making and selling its product for alleged patent infringement while the trial is waiting to begin. Regardless who wins the case, the impact of the injunction on the defendant would be enormous due to the lost production and revenue during the injunction period.

To achieve freedom of operation, traditionally many companies file patents defensively to protect their own products. As previously illustrated, because a granted patent only gives patent owner exclusive rights, it may not give enough protection on the sale of his own products. Then, how does the defense strategy work to achieve freedom of operation?

The defense strategy is built upon the following philosophies:

1. A strong portfolio should be built to prevent injunction or litigation from happening. As previously discussed in Section 2.2, the pyramid is a typical strategy in building a patent portfolio. A good patent portfolio should include a mixture of patents covering all product features with different scope of claims from pioneering to broad system claims to incremental improvements. Such portfolio is proved to be the most prone to attacks. The key to a defense strategy is the right combination of quantity and claim scope.
2. Counter assertion is a very common defensive weapon in today's litigation or assertion cases. If a patent owner sues a manufacturer for

infringing his patents, the manufacturer may consider asserting back with her own patents on the plaintiff's products. This is only possible if both parties make and sell products and the defending party has a good portfolio of her own. Therefore, filing patents for defense is quite important. A defensive portfolio can be turned into an offensive weapon. Before someone asserts or sues anyone, he should assess the counter assertion risk by examining his target company's patent portfolio. Certainly, a company with a strong portfolio has a lower risk of being asserted than a company without.

3. Still, to be able to achieve freedom of operation on one's own product, a product clearance needs to be conducted to make sure there are no patents that may be infringed. If there are any key patents identified as a roadblock to your product, i.e. someone may have already obtained a patent with broader scope that may cover your products, a license-in option may be considered. If you have a strong patent portfolio, you may be able to reach cross-licensing deals with the other party via "trading" of your own patents.

11.3 Offense Strategy

Offense strategy is to actively seek out potential adopters of a patented invention or identify infringers and approach them to force them into taking a license. With the new trend of increased importance of intellectual property in corporate value structures, the offense strategy has been gaining more attention while corporations in the United States have been looking for ways to promote, license and leverage their intellectual property.

For example, Hewlett Packard Company, the leading company in innovation, has been aggressively filing patents to become top 5 companies worldwide to receive a total of close to 9,000 granted U.S. patents during 2003–2007. In comparison to its traditional defense strategy (including cross-licensing) through the 1980's, Hewlett Packard has launched an aggressive strategy in the late 90's to increase their patent filings with the objective of enforcing their intellectual property in core product segments. As the result, the company's intellectual property value has grown seven times in four years.

In order to sustain in the competitive market, the offense strategy is as important as the defense strategy for any company. It is not only a protection for one's products but also viewed by many corporations as a source of revenue.

11.4   The "Carrot" Licensing and the "Stick" Licensing

In the intellectual property licensing field, there are two types of licensing: the carrot licensing and the stick licensing. As self-explained, the carrot licensing refers to a friendly approach in luring the target to adopting one's invention and taking a license. In the stick licensing approach, the patent owner identifies alleged infringer and asserts his patents against the infringer with the attempt of forcing into a license.

From an expert's view, the stick licensing is often more straight-forward once the alleged company using the patent is identified. For stick licensing, much work is done before approaching the target company including effort to identify target companies and products and collecting evidence of use. On the other hand, the effort associated with the carrot licensing approach is usually made after approaching the party. By then, one will attempt to convince the party of the advantages of the invention and persuade them to adopt it.

There are different scenarios when the carrot or the stick licensing is more suitable than the other. If a patent is still at its early age where there is no evidence of market use, it would make sense to take the carrot licensing approach to promote the invented technology and find early adopters. If the technology is more mature and if there is already a market use of it, it would make sense to take the stick licensing approach and directly approach infringers to force them into negotiation. In fact, many companies are willing to negotiate the assertion case to avoid high legal cost associated with potential litigations.

11.5   Patent Issues in Standards

There are numerous standard efforts being initiated each year. Standards are voluntary and consensus based, i.e. the participation of the standard body is purely voluntary. A participant may have influence on the drafting of technical specification of the standard and rights to vote for the passing of the standard. For each standard, it may take years' efforts to finalize, during which period numerous discussions, drafting, revision, reference implementation and testing are conducted among participants. If so much time and resources have to be spent before a standard is complete, what is the motivation of an organization participating in a standard body? This section attempts to address this question mainly from the intellectual property's standpoint.

11.5.1 *Intellectual Property Management in Standards*

Intellectual property is always a sensitive issue in any standard body. Typically, two guidelines are commonly adopted by most standard bodies:

1. Each participant should have a binding representation that no patents shall stand in the way of the use of the proposed standard. Basically, each participant hands out the rights of their relevant patents to the standard that they become part of the standard patent pool. Each individual participant shall not use their patents to block any nonstandard participants from using the standard and developing standardized products.
2. Each participant will grant users of the standard licenses on Reasonable And Non-Discriminatory (RAND) terms and conditions, for which the royalty rate is usually set by the standard body and applied to the patent pool in whole.

For example, MPEG2 license is being handled by MPEG LA, which has two packages available for license: MPEG2 Video and Systems; and MPEG2 System (without video encoding and decoding). For each package, there is a patent pool contributed by related participants. For example, the patent pool for MPEG2 System is contributed by Alcatel Lucent, GE Technology Development, Inc., Hitachi, Ltd., Koninklijke Philips Electronics N.V., Mitsubishi, Samsung Electronics Co., Ltd.,

Scientific Atlanta and Thomson Licensing[1]. A user wishing to deploy MPEG2 systems only needs to do one-stop shop at MPEG LA to license all essential patents covering MPEG2 systems.

Therefore, participating in a standard can be a lucrative business if one has some essential patents and the standard has been widely adopted. Is that the only reason a company should join the standard body and is there any downside participating in a standard?

11.5.2 *Considerations in Standard Participation*

The future financial return from licensing intellectual property is certainly the main driving force for a company to participate in a standard body. But it should not be the only consideration. As a matter of fact, some standard bodies make clear policy of RAND-Zero regarding intellectual property, i.e. the adoption of the standard is royalty-free to all users. There shall be other considerations to be taken into account before one decides to participate in a standard:

1. A clear vision on the standard in terms of whether it will succeed and gain wide adoption from the industry, and whether the company is planning to be an early adopter. If the answer is positive, the benefits of participating will be:
    a. An advantageous position in intellectual property as previously discussed.
    b. The influence of company's product features, architectures, designs, user interface etc. to the standard. A close alignment of the standard with a company's existing products and know-how will benefit the company with ease-of-deployment of the new standard and shorter time-to-market for their standardized products.
    c. A wider market acceptance of the company's products. For any products complying with the standard, consumers do not have to worry about buying products with

---

[1] Source: MPEG LA at http://www.mpegla.com.

      proprietary technologies that may create incompatibility issues with other brand products.

2. The up-front cost in comparison to the investment return and benefit as discussed above.

3. The risk associated with participating a standard body for the company almost has to "donate" their patents to the pool for either a RAND or RAND-Zero license. If a company has a strong portfolio in related areas, it is advised to consider the possibility of staying out of standard participation thus maintaining the freedom of asserting each individual users of the standard later on. If a company is already participating in the standard, it cannot assert any users of the standard with its own patents because that will violate the intellectual property policy of the standard body.

To conclude this section, from patent transaction perspective, a patent put up for sale or licensing would be a lot more valuable if it reads on a standard yet is not part of the standard patent pool. The obvious reason is that the patent owner is not obliged to any policies of the standard body and has a great control over what he wants to do with the patent. Should the patent owner choose to enforce his patent, the target companies can be easily identified, i.e. the manufacturers of the standardized products. On the other hand, if a patent is already part of the standard patent pool, the power of this enforcing right will be diminished because the patent is available for anyone to license on a RAND term from the patent pool.

11.6   Patent Issues in Open Source

One may ask: if we develop everything using open source, why would we still need to file patents? In order to answer this question, let us take a look at what is covered and warranted by open source and what open source means to your business today.

11.6.1   *Open Source Background and Benefits*

The history of open source software movement goes back to 1980's with the formation of the Free Software Foundation ("FSF") and the release of a series of programs in source code form under the name GNU and its General Public License (GPL). For many years, the open source community filled a relatively small niche in a large and growing market for proprietary products from large companies such as UNIX operating system offered by SUN and Hewlett-Packard. It was not until recently that new "open source" projects would exist in the mainstream of the commercial software market. More recently, the embedded Linux started emerging into the consumer market for embedded and portable devices such as set-top boxes, PDAs and mobile phones.

What does open source mean to your business? To put it simply, open source OS offers an alternative to the monopoly such as Microsoft OS that requires companies paying high licensing fees. Particularly, among many benefits, the company taking an open source license will:

1. Have free access to the source code from a common source code pool, which gives the community an opportunity for speedy project developments.
2. Be granted a broad license, which allows licensees to use, modify and redistribute open source programs. Commercial programs distributed in open source will allow developers to have direct access to the source code and SDK thus provide value added features.

11.6.2 *Open Source Concerns*

The benefits seem to be enticing enough for a company to pursue in the open source direction for their commercial products. However, several concerns have been raised in the past in light of using open source for the deployment of commercial products. These issues are summarized and listed as below.

1. Many open source projects are really more of the product of weekend and after-hours hobbyists and do not enjoy the same code quality and rigorous testing protocol as commercial products. Without contractual warranties from the contributor, the risk falls upon the licensee that the software may contain fatal errors, bugs or other problems that may cause downstream financial consequences.

2. Typically, the open source license does not include any intellectual property representations, warranties or indemnities in favor of the licensee. The license is generally favorable and protective of the contributor that it contains a broad disclaimer of all warranties that benefits the licensor/contributors.

Therefore, it would be a huge risk for any commercial software vendors to indemnify their users because the content covered under such responsibility traces back all the way to the beginning of the open source chain, from whoever provides it or modifies it but there are no contributors who will indemnify the licensee.

11.6.3 *GPL Version 3*

The latest GPL license Version 3 was released in June 2007, 17 years since GPL Version 2. The new GPL license attempted to address the concerns regarding intellectual property. The major addition to Version 3 (v3) is that when someone distributes software covered by GPL v3 that they have written or modified, they must provide every recipient with any patent licenses necessary to exercise the rights that the GPL gives them. The FSF claims that for users and developers working with software covered under GPL v3 they should not worry about a desperate contributor suing them for patent infringement later.

The GPL v3 seems to have addressed the intellectual property concern, but not entirely. The concerns regarding intellectual property are still not addressed in the new version. Particularly,

1. There are still no warranties on any work distributed.
2. The patent license policy only provides covenant not to sue from the distributor but not from any third parties. In other words, there is still no indemnification to the licensee on any patent infringement brought by a third party. Further, if a contributor has modified other people's work therefore is not the original author, his patent license to the user will not cover any work done by the original author.
3. There is an indemnification clause in the GPL v3, but it only applies to the contributor to free them from being sued by any users of their work.

From intellectual property perspective, deploying a product based on open source software is at your own risk. The open source license gives licensees access to the source code and its copyright but does not indemnify the licensee from infringing any third party's intellectual property rights as the result of using open source codes. For any vendor deploying open source programs, the liability of intellectual property should be treated independently from open source standard and positioned as if the company is developing the software on their own.

11.7   Uncovering of Infringing Products

Whether you are an independent inventor or are employed and invent for your employer, you should be on the look-out for any unauthorized use of your invention on the market to catch any possible infringers. This is not your legal obligation but rather it is in your interest to assist any commercialization effort with respect to your own invention. Patent infringement is a legal matter; however, to initially uncover infringers or identify infringed products it often requires highly technical skills of someone understanding the patent and having a vision of the patent's applicable uses. Such experts for this purpose would actually be the inventors themselves like you.

Like documenting and keeping a lab book for your own invention (as discussed in Chapter 6), uncovering infringement also requires collecting evidence and documenting your findings. A hunch that someone's product is infringing your patent is not enough. Collecting evidence, analyzing evidence and developing your proof are essential steps in making your investigation productive and effective so that it may help launch any successful assertion or litigation against infringers.

The following gives you several tips in infringement detection:

1. The evidence of use must be compared with your claims to determine infringement. I often hear inventors say that someone is using their invention, but once they take a close look at their claims they find out that their claims are made narrower than described in the specification therefore an infringement case will not hold.

2. You can be aggressive in making assumptions of someone's infringement and go prove it, but you must be honest and treat your investigation as serious as scientific research and experiments. Collecting evidence must be done legally.
3. The evidence of use can come from many sources such as the operation of real products, reverse engineering, information from the Internet, patent applications, journals and published papers and product brochures.
4. Work with your legal counsel or management throughout the investigation.

Catching an infringer, whether willful or nonwillful, is not immoral. You do not need to be shy about it. Any patent owner is entitled to his exclusive rights and if you are shy about catching infringers, your infringer will end up being the party making profits out of your invention.

Chapter 12

Patent Evaluation and Patent Maintenance

As an inventor, your company has probably already asked you to evaluate a patent for various purposes such as patent maintenance, patent licensing or sales and patent litigation. In fact, a great deal of inputs usually comes from inventors. Throughout this chapter, various basic elements in patent evaluation will be introduced and explained. Patent maintenance is essentially a patent evaluation process with its own special purpose; therefore, patent maintenance will also be discussed at the end of this chapter.

12.1 Patent Use

Patent use refers to whether the technology in the patent under evaluation is being used. Table 12.1 lists what kind of information should be collected when looking for any patent use.

Patent use is a critical consideration in patent evaluation. It mainly concerns with whether the technology disclosed in the patent is being used in any products or standards, and if not, what is the likelihood that the technology will be used in the near future. If a patent is not being used or unlikely to be used in the future, the value of the patent would be low.

The challenge of identifying uses of patents in other company's products or standards is how to find out these companies or standards in the first place. As an inventor, because you know the insight of the technology and keep abreast of the latest development, you may name a few competitors or related standards as your target and explore any evidence to support your hypothesis of use. If resource is available, you should also work with intellectual property professionals such as patent attorneys, patent portfolio managers or subject matter experts experienced in IP issues and expand your range of targets by identifying applicable markets.

Table 12.1 Considerations of patent use.

	Current Use	Future Use
Company's own products	Is the technology being used or has it been used in any of company's products?	Is the technology being planned for, likely to be planned for or has high applicability to company's future products?
Other company's products	Has the technology been licensed to any companies and which products? Do you believe if any companies are using the technology?	Is the technology likely to be interested to any company and if so, which company and which of their product line?
Standards	Is the technology being included in any standards? If so, is it described in which section and which standard, and is it an essential or optional part of the standard?	Is any standard likely to include the technology in the future? If so, which standard body and what is the time frame of the release of the standard?

Being able to come up with viable target companies requires experience and knowledge, but this is an important skill to possess for an inventor and the reward is high. Being able to identify applicable market and target companies not only helps with patent evaluation, but also supports infringement analysis and assertion for bringing more licensing opportunities.

12.2 Market Potential

If a patent is being used or is likely to be used in the future, knowing the current or potential market size is vital to the patent evaluation or any other strategic decisions with respect to patent. The patent use and its market size directly affect the calculation of royalty and licensing revenue of a patent.

Depending on the evaluation context, the market data may not need to be precise. Rather, an educated guess often suffices. An exemplary definition of windows for your estimate is: < US$10M, between US$10M and US$100M; and > US$100M. There are numerous free websites and report that may help with some preliminary data to make your educated guess. You will need to estimate the current market size and project future market size. The market size should be specific to each country the patent is issued or has a foreign counterpart[1].

12.3 Claim Quality

One of the important criteria in evaluating a patent is how much protection the patent will give to its owner, perspective licensee or buyer. This is determined by the quality of patent claims. With respect to claims, two metrics are primarily being evaluated: claim breadth and claim diversity.

<u>Claim breadth</u> rates the quality of the claim language being used in the patent, i.e. how professional and solid is the claim language employed. As discussed in Chapter 4, the broadest claim of a patent is its independent claim. To evaluate a patent's claim breadth, you will need to read all its independent claims and determine if they can be expected to support a broad construction scope. Also look for any key limiting step/element or phrase that may significantly impact any future use of claims.

For more extensive patent evaluation, very often, patent prosecution history will be examined to make sure there is nothing in the responses to Office Action that may have narrowed the scope of the invention from what appears in the claim. The analysis on the scope of the invention and

---

[1] A foreign counterpart or a foreign family is a patent filed in another country based on the same invention filed at its home country. The foreign counterpart claims the same priority date of the parent patent. As will be described in Chapter 15, the USPTO PAIR or esp@cenet are good sources of finding family members of a patent.

prosecution history has already been discussed in Chapters 4 and 8, respectively.

Claim diversity refers to how many ways the novel features are claimed. The meaning to this is twofold. One is the variety of different types of claims with similar scope. An algorithm can be made into a method claim or a system employing every step of the method. A patent having a good variety of claim types gives better choice and protection in freedom of operation than a single independent claim does.

The other meaning to claim diversity is the claiming of a feature in a number of ways that will catch different types of infringers. This has been illustrated in Section 7.5. From licensing point of view, a patent with diversified claims may enable its owner to draw more attention from potential users operating in somewhat but not entirely overlapped space as claimed in the patent.

12.4 Technical Strength

Technical strength refers to how fundamental the technology in the patent stands in its field. The following questions should be answered in assessing the technical strength of a patent:

1. Is the technology essential in solving the problem in the field that there is no work around? If a patent reads on any mandatory portion of a standard, it is considered essential.
2. Can the technology in the patent emerge as a new business in the future?
3. If the technology is already implemented, how difficult is it to design around? This is often indicative of how effective a patent can be used for licensing. If someone is caught using the patent without obtaining a license, he might consider either taking a license or designing around the patent. The design around has to do with both the technical merit of the patent and cost associated with implementing it. Particularly,
    a. The technical merit of a patent allows its licensees to make differentiating products among all competitors for

its technical superiority and efficiency. If someone has to design around it, he will definitely sacrifice the efficiency and lose its technical advantage to some extent or entirely.

b. The difficulty of design around also has to do with the cost associated with altering the invented technology in order to get around the patent. The cost for altering the invention may be attributable to its engineering development cost. It may also be associated with the social impact on existing customers. Specifically, if it is a graphical user interface patent, it may be easy to modify the code to get around. However, while many existing customers are already tuned to the look and feel of the product, will the change of user interface turn these customers away? This adverse effect is an indirect cost to the design around.

12.5   Ease of Detection and Reverse Engineering Cost

The ease of detection refers to how easy it is to detect infringement. Again, a patent pertaining to a special icon in a graphical user interface would be very easy to detect. On the other hand, if a patent is about a color enhancement algorithm inside a digital camera, it would be very difficult to detect. In order to detect how the algorithm is done inside the camera, one would have to look inside the chip in the device and reverse engineer the code to prove it, which is extremely difficult, and costly too.

If the detection is easy or the cost of reverse engineering (to prove infringement) is low, it will definitely deter infringers and lure them to take a license of the patent. Such patents will be highly desirable.

12.6   Surrounding Patents

As discussed in Chapter 2, a pyramid patent portfolio with a diverse mixture of patents in the same technology gives much stronger protection than a single patent does. One measure to be taken in evaluating a patent for the purpose of licensing, sales or maintenance, is to find out whether or not the patent is part of a surrounding patent of a larger portfolio. If a patent is a surrounding patent, even if it is not being used anywhere or does not have a broad scope of protection, it may still have some perks. Quantity counts as a negotiating power for all patent licensing and acquisition transactions.

12.7 Patent Enforceability

For patent evaluation associated with patent sales, licensing or litigation, patent enforceability is essential as the patent must be in force in order to be sold, licensed or litigated. Major concerns regarding enforceability include:

1. Is maintenance fee paid up? During the life of a patent, maintenance fees must be paid to the USPTO in order for the patent to stay in force. If the maintenance fee lapses, a patent will expire. Patent maintenance will be explained in the next section.
2. Is there any potential invalidity issues? Any patents under consideration for sales or licensing should be scrutinized against any potential invalidity issues. Such issues refer to the likelihood or any indication that the patent may be invalidated for any reason in the future. A patent is assumed to be valid[2] unless it is being otherwise challenged by another party and determined by the USPTO or the court. Examples of basis for challenging the validity of a patent include:
   a. Any evidence of "public use or on sale in this country" more than one year prior to the patent's filing date. This relates to 102 rejection as previously discussed in Chapter 9. However, it is usually overlooked at the USPTO during the prosecution stage for it is not possible for an examiner to explore the market use of a specific technology for all patents being examined.

---

[2] Patent Law 35 U.S.C. 282: "A patent shall be presumed valid. Each claim of a patent (whether in independent, dependent, or multiple dependent form) shall be presumed valid independently of the validity of other claims; ... The burden of establishing invalidity of a patent or any claim thereof shall rest on the party asserting such invalidity."

b. Any challenge on statutory disclosure requirement. Basically, most of the patent laws and requirements pertaining to obtaining a patent, as discussed previously in this book, can be challenged. Anyone interested in a patent for potential purchase or license should look for any obvious flaw that may exist in the patent such as "best mode", "enablement" etc.

c. Inventorship and inequitable conduct. There are case laws and studies provided early in Sections 3.6 and 10.1 to illustrate the importance of correct inventorship and publications post patent granting.

3. Is there any prior art risk? This question can often be answered by a technical expert familiar with the art pertaining to the invention. The expert will assess whether the invention was truly state of the art at the time of the filing. Also, any evidence of "patents or published patent applications" prior to the patent's filing date can raise prior art issues. For the same reason mentioned before, this may likely be overlooked during the prosecution stage as no one can expect any examiner to do an exhaustive search particularly on publications. Sometimes, a patent with a late priority date or too broad claims may trigger speculations or concerns over prior art risk.

In summary, considerations associated with patent evaluation include all technical (technical quality, design around, ease of detection and reverse engineering), legal (claim quality) and business (market potential, surrounding patent) aspects. Having a clear picture of these metrics is a must in conducting due diligence for any patent transactions.

12.8   About Patent Maintenance

Patent maintenance refers to paying a series of fees to the USPTO during the life of a patent[3] in order to keep the patent in force. Because there are fees associated with maintaining a patent, patent owner shall make

---

[3] Maintenance fee is only applicable to utility patents from applications filed on or after December 12, 1980.

decisions, at each time the fee is due, as to whether or not to continue paying maintenance fee to keep the patent current.

Patent maintenance is only required for utility patents. At the issuance of a patent, the patent owner pays the issue fee (US$720 for small entity), which is good for the next three and half years. During the life of a patent, a patent owner needs to continue paying patent maintenance fee at three scheduled windows: 3 ½, 7 ½ and 11 ½ years from the date the patent is granted in order to keep the patent in force. Failure to pay the maintenance fee on time may result in the expiration of the patent therefore the abandonment of all legal rights associated with it. A patent with a lapse of maintenance fee will become un-licensable or un-salable.

At current fee schedule, patent maintenance fees for small entities are: US$465, US$1180 and US$1955 for 3 ½, 7 ½ and 11 ½ year window, respectively. Small entities are usually a nonprofit organization, universities and government, or for-profit organization under 500 employees. Entities not satisfying the criteria defined in the Patent Rule[4] are subject to pay large entity fee, which is exactly double the amount of those for small entities. If the above fees are added up, the total cost of owning a utility patent (including issue fee) can be as high as US$4500 if it is owned by a small entity and $9000 if owned by a large entity.

The last payment of patent maintenance fee, which covers the last five years of a patent, is the highest and most significant portion of revenue for the PTO. However, this is greatly affected by the fluctuations in the patent maintenance decisions made by the owners. Statistically, 79% of patent owners pay their first maintenance fee at 3 ½ year; 55% of patent owners pay their second fee at 7 ½ year and only 32% pay their last maintenance fee[5].

Therefore, from business perspective, patent owners do make decisions at various stages of the life of a patent. The criteria applied to patent maintenance decision are based on the metrics used for patent evaluation except patent invalidity and prior risk assessment. Patent

---

[4] 37 CFR 1.27.

[5] David A. Burge, "Patent and Trademark Tactics and Practice", John Wiley & Sons, Inc. 1999.

invalidity and prior art risk are being evaluated more often by parties other than patent owners for patent sale, licensing or litigation purposes.

As an inventor, if you are requested to evaluate your patent for maintenance purpose, be honest with your assessment. Being an inventor of a patent is certainly an honor and pride. Dropping the patent from the maintenance list, however, does not remove this pride. Your patent is still published and public accessible at the USPTO or any other patent databases. Evaluating a patent requires true assessment on the merits and no personal attachment to the process.

The final business decision on patent maintenance should be a combined evaluation based on all the above considerations, as well as the budget situation of each patent owner.

Chapter 13

Patent Sales, Licensing and Common Practices

Patent sales and licensing are common ways of capitalizing a patent asset and are completely different industries from their creations, i.e. patent filing and prosecution. Patent filing and prosecution are usually handled by patent attorneys and agents, whereas patent sales and licensing are usually handled by patent brokerage firms or sometimes directly handled by the patent owner himself. This chapter aims to give readers some exposure to what is being generally concerned in a patent sales or licensing transaction. Such greater insight will give you a broader perspective when you are dealing with patents at different stages.

13.1 Outright Sale or Licensing

When deciding to capitalize a patent asset, patent owners often face the decision whether to sell the asset or license it. There are two primary factors to consider:

1. Is the asset part of the company's core business? If not, you may consider to sell it outright, i.e. to completely give up all the rights. The downside of selling it outright is that you may completely lose control without knowing who might be subsequently taking a license from the buyer or whom the patent may be sold to later. If it is still part of your company's core business and you are facing competitors in the market segment, you would want to select the licensing route, which will definitely give you more control with respect to who might be using the invented technology.

2. There are other financial considerations to take into account. For example, selling it outright may give you more cash up front. On the other hand, licensing may let you collect more money from royalties in the long run. Particularly, if you are able to give nonexclusive license to multiple parties, your income multiplies.

A few things are noteworthy:

License grant back. If you decide to sell your patent while still in operation using the invented technology or want to keep that option for the future, you may ask for a grant back license to be included in the deal, for which you will get a nonexclusive perpetual license from the buyer. This license will keep you to continue operating in the business.

Non-exclusive and exclusive license. Nonexclusive license is very common and more preferred, for which the patent owner may give license to multiple parties and not stuck with only one licensee. This maximizes the opportunity for capital return.

Exclusive license with enforcement rights. Sometimes the seller is constrained with their rights to the asset and cannot sell outright. This is particularly true with patents developed under government funding. One exercise is that the patent owner grants a nonexclusive license with enforcement rights (for litigation) to the licensee. This is in some sense equivalent to outright sales and actually leaves the patent owner with no power, but on the paper (USPTO record) there is no transfer of rights or change of ownership.

13.2　Bundling and Field of Use

One thing that must be defined in either sales or licensing deal is the content of the asset and the scope of usage (of the patent asset), which defines the market segment to be covered.

Bundling several surrounding patents in similar technologies is a common practice. For any perspective buyer or licensee, he would like to maximize his freedom of action with a bundled asset instead of a single patent. If one is to license a single patent from the seller, he would not want to be sued the next day on the infringement of another patent by the same patent licensor. Therefore, the bundling of similar patents in a transaction is desired and sensible.

The bundling may also apply to any corresponding foreign patents (or called foreign family or foreign counterparts) as well as patents involved in double patenting and terminal disclaimer[1]. If one patent is granted upon the filing of a terminal disclaimer that refers to an earlier patent to the same inventor, this earlier patent is preferred to be included in the deal otherwise the second patent becomes much less enforceable.

The patent or the bundle of patents in consideration for a licensing transaction naturally defines the scope of operation for the licensee. However, in practice, the scope, or the field of use is often clearly defined in the licensing agreement to minimize any unforeseen usage of the patent if any. Although a patent claim is made in the context disclosed in the specification, a patent may turn out to be a hidden treasure such that the same claim may be applicable to an unforeseeable industry in the future. For example, a patent on facsimile communication during the late 80's or early 90's may turn out to be applicable to more recent Internet based communication without explicit mentioning of Internet communication in the original specification. In order to protect this "undeveloped" space, it is therefore particularly important for the licensor to define the field of use in a foreseeable industry segment in the context while keeping licensing rights of other unforeseeable industry segments as future opportunities.

---

[1] Terminal disclaimer is a USPTO procedure that often allows an applicant to overcome an obviousness rejection of his application based on the same invention by the same applicant (double patenting). By applicant filing a terminal disclaimer, the second patent will be allowed.

13.3   Patent Ownership

Unlike real estate business, there is no title insurance for patent sales. It is therefore extremely important for any buyer or licensee to verify the ownership (title) of the patent. It is also equally important for a patent owner to keep a record of clean title or chain of titles in order to satisfy any potential buyers or licensees. With respect to patent titles, both patent owners/licensors and perspective buyers/licensees need to be aware of several issues to be described in the remainder of this section.

13.3.1   *Chain of Titles*

A patent can be sold once, twice or any number of times. The so-called chain of titles refers to a complete record of change of ownership during the life of a patent. The chain should start from the inventor and record any change of ownership in the following typical scenarios:

1. All patents are originally the property of the inventor. If there is a pre-existing contractual obligation of the inventor to transfer the ownership of a patent to his employer, there should be a record of assignment from the inventor to the company per invention.
2. If a company is acquired or changes its name, there should be a record reflecting the new name of the patent owner.
3. If a patent is sold, there should be a record of new assignment and transfer of rights.
4. If a company is dissolved or undergoes bankruptcy, there should be a settlement on who the new owner of the patent is and a record reflecting such.

All documents related to the chain of titles should be recorded with the USPTO. The acceptance by the USPTO and subsequent release of such record in the USPTO PAIR system is an indication that original documents or certified true copies were submitted to the USPTO. This gives any potential buyer a high degree of assurance of the ownership of the patent in question.

13.3.2 *Government Regulations*

If a patent is conceived while conducting research under government funding, the patent owner needs to be prudent on what rights he has because each government agency has specific regulations pertaining to intellectual properties, data rights and computer software. In order to establish clear ownership of a patent, any government interest must be examined closely in accordance with the appropriate regulations. There are commonly three regulations pertaining to intellectual property that involve government contracts:

Bayh-Dole Act[2] concerns intellectual property arising from federal government funded research at university, nonprofit organization and small business. Among many things, it allows government contractors to retain the title of the intellectual property in exchange for granting the federal government a nonexclusive, nontransferable, irrevocable, royalty-free license for government's purpose. The motives of Bayh-Dole Act are to promote commercialization of technologies, continued research and education. In practice, in order for a government contractor to retain a clear title to the invention, certain guidelines need to be followed under the provisions of the Act. Examples of provisions include reporting inventions to the federal funding agency, sharing royalties with the inventors, giving preference to universities and small businesses etc.

Federal Acquisition Regulations (FAR) and Defense Federal Acquisition Regulations Supplements (DFARS) address ownership issues of intellectual property rights generated by a government contractor and are governing most government agencies. Under FAR and DFARS, similar to Bahy-Dole Act, the title of the patent developed under a government contract can be retained by the contractor subject to a royalty free license to the government. The FAR and DFARS also provide government with Limited Rights or Unlimited Rights for any technical data and software depending on the contract. The copyright of computer software

---

[2] Patent Law 35 USC 200–202.

developed under the contract can be retained by the contractor with the permission from the contracting officer at the government agency.

A critical issue relating to any government funding regulation is the determination of whether the patent is covered by any government regulation (referred to "subject invention" category). Typically, any invention developed or conceived prior to the government contract shall belong to the contractor. Any invention conceived or first implemented in the performance of work under the contract will fall into the "subject invention" category and is subject to the above government regulation.

13.4 Litigation History

Another common place to look in association with patent sales or licensing consideration is the litigation history of the patent. There are commercial databases such as Lexis-Nexis that provides tools to search for such information. Whether or not a patent has been litigated in the past and the details and status of the litigation may affect how the patent is viewed in future sales or licensing. For example, if a patent was involved in a litigation, whether it wins or loses in the court directly affects the strength and enforceability of the patent for its future use.

Chapter 14

Patent Valuation

We have talked about patent evaluation in Chapter 12. To refresh, patent evaluation is the assessment of a patent in its quality and potential opportunity for licensing and sales. Patent valuation, on the other hand, is about the pricing of a patent. It is largely based on the outcome of patent evaluation.

The goal of this chapter is to introduce interested readers to patent valuation and give some statistics on patent auctions and patent infringement damage awards in past litigations. Through an introduction of key processes in patent valuation, this chapter helps you understand what is important in patent valuation. In doing so, it helps direct your effort into augmenting the potential value of your innovation through development of a proper patent strategy at its various stages.

14.1 Intangible Assets and Why Valuation

Unlike fixed assets such as manufacturing facilities, office equipment and furniture etc., intangible assets do not physically exist, but they are still valuable to the success of a business. Examples of intangible assets include patents, trademarks, brand names, customer or distribution networks, and technical know-how etc. Patents and trademarks are also considered as subsets of intellectual property.

In the past, when a company's intellectual property asset was viewed in connection with its revenue, patents were not paid much attention. However, recently, they have been regarded more. For example, the majority of high tech companies were filing patents with the focus on defensive needs and protection of their products. Until recently, when dissolving distressed companies, many VCs focused mostly on consolidating fixed and tangible assets, neglecting patent assets. As the result of increased awareness of intellectual property in recent years, patents are no longer just the topic of interest to inventors, scientists and patent attorneys; they have also drawn interests from business people, investors and financial players. Today, many efforts in monetizing patents are seen mainly in the following contexts:

1. "Digging hidden treasures" from long inactive intellectual property assets and monetizing them.
2. Launching aggressive licensing program with the attempt to bring in additional revenue to compensate for R&D cost or other license-in expenses.
3. With the shift of business objectives selling intellectual property assets that no longer relate to company's core business.
4. Selling intellectual property assets in connection with bankruptcies and dissolving of distressed companies, and often using patents instead of fixed assets in leveraging a transaction.
5. Spending more resource on consulting services for evaluating and pricing intellectual property assets in merger-and-acquisition (M&A) transactions.
6. Donating to charity, for the purpose of tax relief, company's intellectual property assets that are not foreseen to be used in the future.

There is no doubt that insight on the value of intellectual property assets is desired in any of the above various contexts and transactions regarding patents. Without any monetary figures, no properties can be measured, valued or traded. Because of complex issues involved in various business transactions of patent assets, patent valuation itself deserves a book of its own. Patent valuation is an art of business and requires multitude of skills in legal, business, technical and finance. In this chapter, we attempt to shed some lights on this topic via brief introduction of some popular approaches for patent valuation without diving into details in each context of business transactions.

14.2 Representative Valuation Approaches

Several classical patent valuation approaches will be described below. Each technique has its pros and cons and can be more suitable for one business transaction than the other, depending on the type and complexity of business transactions.

14.2.1 *Cost Approach*

The cost approach answers the question: "How much does it cost to develop the asset?" This method assesses the value of a patent asset by measuring the expenditures necessary to replace the asset. The primary contributors of this cost are patent related R&D cost, plus other related costs in:

1. Application/registration fees and attorney fees associated with the filing.
2. Personnel costs.
3. Development and production costs.
4. Marketing and advertising costs.
5. Other legal fees.

From patent owner's perspective, the cost method gives him an absolute minimum value for the asset in order to break it even. If the asset is sold under this minimum value, it will be sold below the cost. If such scenario occurs, the patent owner needs to make his decision whether to sell it for under the cost while still get some return on the investment or not to sell it hoping to wait for better opportunities. This is often a decision that is to be based on many factors like the age of the asset (how much longer can you wait before the patent expires), the direction that the market is heading to (whether the market is moving towards or away from the invention) and the budget situation in the company (whether the company is in need of cash).

From a purchaser's (licensee's) perspective, the cost approach is basically based on the economic principle of substitution and essentially he should pay no more than what it would cost him to develop himself.

Therefore, the cost approach should derive a max to the perspective buyer or licensee.

The cost method does not reflect the economic benefit derived from owning or using the asset. Nor does it reflect the earning potential of the asset. The cost approach is often used when a patent asset is still at its early stage and no specific market use or market size is available.

14.2.2   *Income Approach*

The income approach answers the question: "How much are we going to earn with this patent in the next 10 years?" This method attempts to determine the future revenues the patent holder is expected to earn by using his patent. The primary contributors to this approach are the following parameters:

1. Projection of the size of the market that the patent asset is pertaining to.
2. Affected market size attributable to the claims (exclusive rights) of a specific patent and discounted future revenue projection.
3. Duration of future income stream – how many years can the patent holder enjoy using the patent?
4. Risks associated with the generation of future revenue (e.g. risks associated with assertion).

Although the income approach is based on the estimate of the market and may seem less precise than the cost approach, there are numerous information sources, free or fee-based market reports, and systematic approaches available to accurately develop and verify both existing and future market. Many consulting firms are also available to provide this service.

The challenge for the income approach is the estimate of which part of the products' revenue is related to the exclusive rights of a specific patent. This might be easy for some industries, such as pharmaceutical, where a specific product may be protected by one patent only. In other industries like computer, this estimate might be difficult and time consuming to obtain since a computer is composed of hundreds of components, which are protected by thousands of patents covering a broad spectrum of technology from semiconductor, circuits, hard drives, memory chips to operating system, memory and network management, graphical user interface and software applications.

Income based approach is one of the most widely used approaches for patent valuation because the information about the market size and trends is readily available. An exemplary case study of patent valuation using the income approach will be further illustrated in the next section.

14.2.3 *Market Approach*

The market approach is like traditional comparison sales approach in real estate business: estimates the value of an asset based on previous market sales data. When such previous sale data is available, this approach tends to be the most robust because it shows what the buyer is willing to pay for the asset and what the seller is willing to take at the same time. Therefore, the intangible assets shall be valued by comparing recent sales or other transactions involving similar assets in related markets.

The market approach poses two challenges:

1. It may be difficult to find data of patents which are already priced and traded, particularly data for those similar patents that you can compare with. The strength of market approach is its reliance on the market sales and licensing transactions. In reality, this approach is only reliable when reliable market data can be found. In today's IP marketplace, most patent licensing and sales are carried out in private. In addition, the intellectual property market is still young, and such market data to be sought are generally sparse and much regression analysis is needed to correlate between indicators and values.

2. Every patent is unique and there is no definition what a similar patent is. Even if two patents are describing similar inventions, their claim scopes may be different. How to quantify the difference of claims and how the difference affect the market revenue that is attributable to the patent is a difficult task. Furthermore, just like real estate, two patents can vary in many ways such as the content of invention, patent age, number of claims and claim scope, technical and claim quality etc.

There is no standard chart as to how to adjust the value up and down according to these differences.

The market approach is generally difficult to apply to patent valuation unless the patents for comparison are truly similar and there are mature market data available. On the other hand, this approach can be useful for one single patent owner to compare values of different patents in the same portfolio. One may have sold one patent for $X, and it may be relatively straightforward to estimate the value of another patent of the same owner in the same technology area.

Later in this chapter, we will briefly talk about Ocean Tomo patent auction that gives an example of market data on patents that are publicly traded.

Patent valuation is not a single-price-calculation. Different approaches may be applied to the same patent asset and an adjustment needs to be made to derive the logical basis for the value of a technology opportunity protected by intellectual property — often measured by net present value (NPV). In reality, discounted cash flow NPV is derived from the logical base while considering other factors such as:

1. Competitive factors.
2. Market penetration.
3. Quality of claims and patent portfolio.
4. Prior art risks (e.g. the chance of finding prior art to invalidate the patent in evaluation).
5. Counter assertion risk.
6. Risk of future exposure – the risk associated with not purchasing the portfolio at the current time yet realizing the cost for future settlement of potential assertions or litigations involving possible infringement by the company's present or future products. This is often referred to as defensive value.

Please note that although each patent valuation technique can offer some reference value as to what the patent is worth to one party, but the value may not be the same as viewed from another party for people may be using different approaches and only looking at factors being concerned to them. For example, the seller may be looking at projected revenues while the potential buyer is assessing the risk from defensive side, i.e. if he is not buying now, how much would it cost (later on) should litigation on the infringement of the same patent occur? Ultimately, in order to reach any deals, other factors must be considered and negotiation is needed between patent owners and perspective buyers or licensees.

14.3 Exemplary Case Study of Patent Valuation

This section intends to give you an example in relation to the income approach with respect to how to derive an estimate of market revenue from the product pertaining to the patent(s) in question. Two key questions to be answered in this process are:

1. What percentage of the cost of the product is attributable to the patent asset?
2. What is the affected market revenue of the product being looked at?

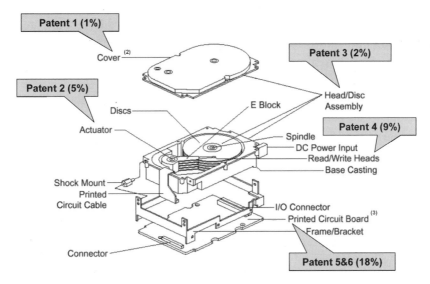

Fig. 14.1 Cost breakdown for patent valuation purpose.

In the example shown in Fig. 14.1, a patent portfolio of six patents is broken down into different technologies that contribute to different parts of the hard drive (HDD). According to the cost of each part relative to the entire HDD, the attributing cost from each patent can be estimated.

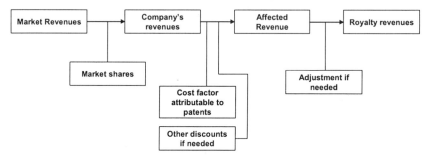

Fig. 14.2 An exemplary patent valuation driver chart.

Furthermore, as shown in Fig. 14.2, a typical patent valuation driver chart is used to derive the royalty revenue, which is estimated based on the revenue of company's product pertaining to the patents being valuated, and further discounted by the cost factor attributable to these patents. In practice, for some patents particularly software patents, while it is difficult to obtain a precise cost attributable to the patents relative to the entire software product, a nominal royalty rate per patent (e.g. 0.25–1%) is sometimes used based on affected revenue, or a 25% rate is applied to licensee's net profit.

It is also worth mentioning the well-known 15 Georgia-Pacific factors to be considered when determining the royalty rate. The short version of the 15 factors is listed below.

1. The royalties received by patent owner for licensing the patent, proving or tending to prove an established royalty.
2. The rates paid by the licensee for the use of other similar patents.
3. The nature and scope of the license, such as whether it is exclusive or nonexclusive, restricted or unrestricted in terms of territory or customers.

4. Patent owner's policy of maintaining its patent monopoly by licensing the use of the invention only under special conditions designed to preserve the monopoly.
5. The commercial relationship between patent owner and licensees, such as whether they are competitors in the same territory in the same line of business or whether they are inventors and promoters.
6. The effect of selling the patented specialty in promoting sales of other products of the patent owner; the existing value of the invention to patent owner as a generator of sales of nonpatented items; and the extent of such derivative or "convoyed" sales.
7. The duration of the patent and the term of the license.
8. The established profitability of the patented product, its commercial success and its current popularity.
9. The utility and advantages of the patent property over any old modes or devices that had been used.
10. The nature of the patented invention, its character in the commercial embodiment owned and produced by the licensor and the benefits to those who used it.
11. The extent to which the infringer used the invention and any evidence probative of the value of that use.
12. The portion of the profit or selling price that is customary in the particular business or in comparable businesses.
13. The portion of the realizable profit that should be credited to the invention as distinguished from any nonpatented elements, manufacturing process, business risks, significant features or improvements added by the infringer.
14. The opinion testimony of qualified experts.
15. The amount that patent owner and a licensee would have agreed upon at the time the infringement began if they had reasonably and voluntarily tried to reach an agreement.

For readers further interested in this topic, please refer to Georgia-Pacific case law[1].

---

[1] Georgia-Pacific Corp. vs. United States Plywood Corp., 318 F. Supp. 1116 [S.D.N.Y.70].

14.4   Patent Auction Pricing Case Study

With respect to the market approach to patent valuation, it can be difficult to gather market data since most patents are privately traded. Furthermore, the patent sales market is generally young, thus, there is no mature market data readily available. What is currently available is the recent Ocean Tomo public patent auction statistics, which will be analyzed in detail in this section.

In the spring of 2006, Ocean Tomo, a Chicago based company, hosted its first public patent auction in San Francisco. It covered primarily patent auctions and some domain name auctions. Since then, Ocean Tomo has been hosting auctions twice a year (the spring and the fall) in the United States. With increased interests in the general public, additional public patent auctions have been held in London, Amsterdam and more are being planned in Hong Kong and Tokyo.

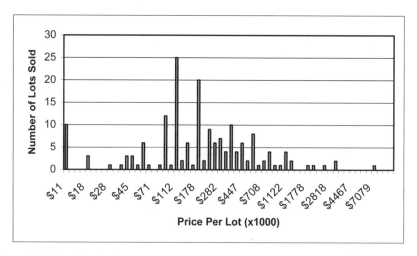

Fig. 14.3 Price distribution of Ocean Tomo patent auction sales. Price is per lot. Data includes five auctions listed in Table. 14.1.

Combining 177 sold lots from last five auctions: Fall 2006, Spring and Fall 2007, Spring and Summer 2008, the price distribution is shown in Fig. 14.3. As seen, the majority of auction lots were sold at US$30K–US$1.2M with the median around US$100K–US$200K range.

Table 14.1 shows a break down of the price for each auction, which indicates that the median price of each auction seems to agree with the overall US$100K–US$200K range whereas the Summer 2008 auction's median price is slightly higher than most other auctions. Furthermore, from statistics on US patents only, the median and average price per patent are around US$100,000 and US$150,000, respectively.

Table 14.1 Ocean Tomo patent auction price per lot.

	Average	Median	Maximum	Minimum
Fall '06	$250,700	$170,000	$900,000	$10,000
Spring '07	$336,147	$134,750	$3,025,000	$11,000
Fall '07	$305,250	$165,000	$1,925,000	$11,000
Spring '08	$370,368	$165,000	$6,600,000	$11,000
Summer '08 (Amsterdam)	$437,036	$224,167	$2,414,104	$43,109

One has to realize that there are some limitations associated with the Ocean Tomo statistics. Particularly,

1. Ocean Tomo patent auctions mainly cover high tech domains including: telecom, multimedia, eCommerce, Internet, Semiconductor, consumer electronics etc. The auctions also cover a few aerospace, automotive and medical device patents. There are no pharmaceutical or life science patents. Therefore, the Ocean Tomo data does not reflect the entire market.
2. The price is not a totally free market price as the minimum price is usually set by the auction rule. Some patents might have been sold below the minimum price yet not included in the statistics.
3. Ocean Tomo runs a screening process for patents to be included in the auction with the attempt to select only patents of high quality and potential interest thus to maximize their own profits. The profits for Ocean Tomo come from 15% of the auction price to be paid by the seller plus 10% paid by the buyer. Therefore, the statistics only reflects what have been selected and subsequently sold in the auction.

To conclude this section, it is noteworthy to mention that any data from Ocean Tomo sales can only give you a snapshot of what the Ocean

Tomo public auction market trend was at the time. You cannot rely on it to price your own patent asset for any future sales as no patents are created equal. In addition, Ocean Tomo patent auctions are mentioned in this section primarily for the widespread availability of its auction results. However, there are many ways of capitalizing a patent asset, both through public and private channels. Ocean Tomo auctions only represent a small portion of the entire market.

14.5   Patent Infringement Damage Statistics

Contrary to the auction price, which is agreed upon at will by both the seller and the buyer, patent infringement damage is set by the court to compensate for the loss that the patent owner has suffered from the infringement regardless whether the defendant has made any profit. The damage amount, or sometimes referred to as award, is calculated based on a complex analysis of the facts and figures presented by both parties.

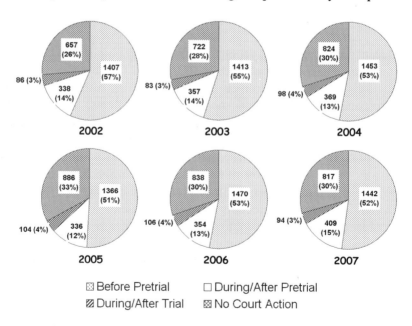

Fig. 14.4 Completed patent cases in U.S. District Courts 2002–2007.

Table 14.2 Top 50 Patent Damage Awards (1980–2007)[2]

Parties	Amount (US$)	Date	Listed Source
Polaroid v. Eastman Kodak	$925,000,000	Jul-91	National Law Journal
City of Hope Medical v. Genentech	$500,000,000	Jun-02	Bloomberg News
InterDigital Communications v. Nokia	$252,000,000	Jan-06	IP Law360
DePuy Spine v. Medtronic	$226,300,000	Sep-07	IP Law360
Haworth v. Steelcase	$211,500,000	Dec-96	Dow Jones
Hughes Tool v. Smith International	$205,000,000	Mar-86	National Law Journal
Bard Peripheral Vascular v. W.L. Gore	$185,000,000	Dec-07	IP Law360
Procter & Gamble v. Paragon Trade	$178,400,000	May-98	PR Newswire
Exxon Chemical v. Mobil Oil	$171,000,000	Aug-98	Houston Chronicle
Masimo v. Nellcor	$164,000,000	Aug-04	IP Law360
z4 Technologies v. Microsoft	$160,000,000	Aug-06	IP Law360
Hughes Aircraft v. United States	$154,000,000	Apr-99	Wall Street Journal
Union Carbide v. Shell Oil	$153,600,000	Oct-05	Reuters
Intergraph v. Intel	$150,000,000	Oct-02	Wall Street Journal
Freedom Wireless v. Boston Communications	$148,100,000	Oct-05	IP Law360
InterDigital Communication v. Samsung	$134,000,000	Sep-06	IP Law360
Rambus v. Hynix Semiconductor	$133,600,000	Jul-06	IP Law360
3M v. Johnson & Johnson	$129,000,000	Dec-92	Dow Jones
Fonar v. General Electric	$128,700,000	Nov-97	Dow Jones
Mobil Oil v. Amoco Chemical	$120,000,000	Sep-98	Business Wire
BJ Services v. Halliburton	$98,100,000	Apr-02	National Law Journal
Honeywell v. Minolta	$96,000,000	Feb-92	Business Week
Unocal v. Six Major Oil Companies	$91,000,000	Mar-00	Yahoo! Finance
U.S. Philips v. KXD Technology	$91,000,000	Oct-07	IP Law360
TIVO v. Echostar Communication	$89,000,000	Oct-06	IP Law360
MuniAuction v. Thomson	$84,600,000	Jul-07	IP Law360
Southern Clay v. United Catalysts	$80,085,157	Apr-01	Court Order
Asyst Technologies v. Empak	$74,700,000	Feb-07	IP Law360
Stryker v. Intermedics Orthopedics	$73,000,000	Sep-96	Reuters
Odetics v. Storage Technology	$70,600,000	Aug-99	Business Wire
General Technology v. Conoco	$68,750,000	Feb-01	National Law Journal
Schneider v. SciMed Life	$68,000,000	Nov-95	Dow Jones
Ariad Pharmaceutical v. Eli Lilly	$65,200,000	May-06	IP Law360

---

[2] Source: FTI Consulting.

Table 14.2 (Continued)

Parties	Amount (US$)	Date	Listed Source
Applied Medical v. Tyco	$64,500,000	Jan-06	IP Law360
Durel v. Osram Sylvania	$63,110,000	Feb-01	National Law Journal
SPX v. Microsoft	$62,300,000	Nov-03	PR Newswire
Harris v. Ericsson	$61,000,000	Nov-02	Texas Blue Sheet
University of Colorado v. American Cyanamid	$57,000,000	Aug-02	National Law Journal
Pfizer v. International Rectifier	$55,800,000	Jul-83	Press Release
Viskase v. American National Can	$54,750,000	Aug-01	Chicago Tribune
LG Philips LCD v. Tatung	$53,500,000	Nov-06	IP Law360
Shiley v. Bentley Laboratories	$53,100,000	Mar-87	Wall Street Journal
800 Adept v. Murex Securities	$49,000,000	Apr-07	IP Law360
Exxon v. Lubrizol	$48,000,000	Nov-93	The Globe and Mail
AcroMed v. Sofamor Danek Group	$47,900,000	Feb-00	National Law Journal
Applied Biosystems v. Micromass	$47,500,000	Apr-02	National Law Journal
Honeywell v. Hamilton Sundstrand	$46,580,000	Mar-01	National Law Journal
TruePosition v. Andrew	$45,300,000	Sep-07	IP Law360
SPX v. Snap-On	$44,000,000	Jan-02	National Law Journal
Studiengesellschaft Kohle v. Dart Industries	$43,765,785	Dec-88	9 USPQ2d 1273

The court has also frequently applied the Georgia-Pacific factors (mentioned early in this chapter) in the award calculation. This section shows some examples of damage amount and some interesting findings in the past litigations.

Table 14.2 shows the top 50 patent damage awards during the past litigations covering all industries. The awarding of patent infringement damage amount to the patent holder is equivalent to the defendant taking a license so they can continue operating, but the patent infringement damage amount is usually significantly higher than what a patent would sell for. The reason is simple: patent sale is a normal business transaction just like the trading of any goods at will, whereas patent infringement is a law suit that is being handled by the U.S. District Court or Federal Circuit, and involves much more efforts by attorneys. It is a much more expensive route. If the damage award was not sufficiently attractive, a plaintiff would not have taken a chance to bring the case to a legal action.

Instead, the plaintiff or both parties may attempt to settle the case before the court trial begins.

As a matter of fact, statistically only a small percentage of law suits filed have gone through the whole process and reached to the end. A statistics on completed patent cases in the U.S. District Courts during the fiscal years 2002–2007[3] is shown in Fig. 14.4. As can be seen, the majority of litigations (over 50%) resulted in their settlements even before the court pretrials begin. The private settlement allows both parties to avoid costly legal fees and at the same time is an enticement for patent owner to get quick cash payment.

---

[3] Source: FTI Consulting. Fiscal year ends September 30th. Original source: Administrative Office of the U.S. Courts.

Chapter 15

Patent Search

Many people think that inventors need to conduct patent search only to determine the patentability of their invention. As a matter of fact, patent search is needed in every stage of the patent value chain: from inventing to strategy and commercialization.

Nowadays with the convenience of Internet and many readily available patent database tools, free or otherwise, patent search is no longer patent law firms' territory. Patent search should be a basic skill of everyone involved in the intellectual property field. Depending on the size and nature of your job, there are a variety of tools that allow you to accomplish both simple and complex patent search tasks. This chapter intends to give you a brief introduction of several patent search or related tools to help you accomplish various tasks described earlier in this book.

15.1 U.S. Patent Search Basics

The basic patent search function is offered in every single patent database tool. This section attempts to give you a brief introduction of the two most popular patent databases: the USPTO and Google database, and highlight key patent search functions of each tool.

15.1.1 USPTO Patent Database

The USPTO patent database is a complete free web-based tool that allows you to search for all U.S. granted patents and published patent applications. You can find it at http://patft.uspto.gov/ or go to USPTO home page at http://www.uspto.gov and look for "patents" → "search patents". The database offers powerful searching functions to help you accomplish sophisticated patent search tasks.

Quick Search

The Quick Search, as illustrated in Fig. 15.1 provides an intuitive graphical user interface that allows you to search by patent number, inventor name, assignee name, U.S. or International class and all other close to 30 fields. This search function also offers Boolean combination of any of the two fields or all fields together.

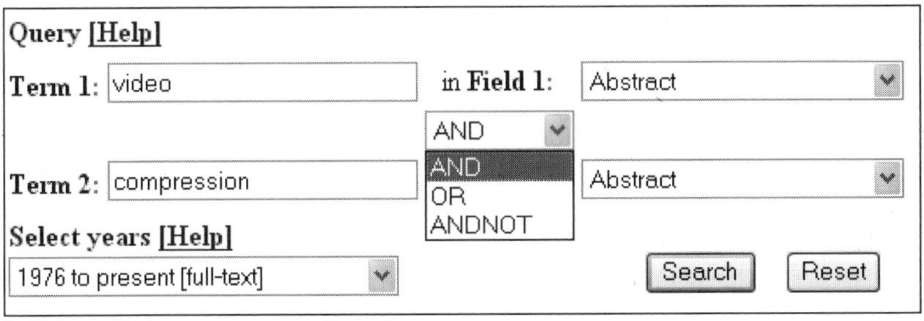

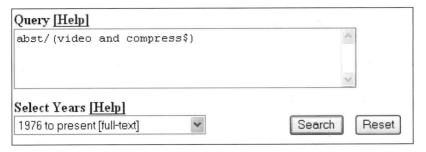

Fig. 15.1 USPTO patent database Quick Search function.

Fig. 15.2 USPTO patent database Advanced Search function.

Advanced Search

Alternatively, user has a choice of using Advanced Search that can accomplish all searching functions in Quick Search, plus more. The Advanced Search, as illustrated in Fig. 15.2, requires user to enter a text query manually in a pre-defined query syntax, which is explained well in the help page of the USPTO database. The Advanced Search requires a little learning curve but it is not difficult to learn at all. Once you grasp it, the Advanced Search can be quite powerful. It will be quite handy and faster to enter your query than Quick Search.

Table 15.1 USPTO Advanced Search field names.

Field Code	Field Name	Field Code	Field Name
PN	Patent Number	IN	Inventor Name
ISD	Issue Date	IC	Inventor City
TTL	Title	IS	Inventor State
ABST	Abstract	ICN	Inventor Country
ACLM	Claim(s)	LREP	Attorney or Agent
SPEC	Description/Specification	AN	Assignee Name
CCL	Current US Classification	AC	Assignee City
ICL	International Classification	AS	Assignee State
APN	Application Serial Number	ACN	Assignee Country
APD	Application Date	EXP	Primary Examiner
PARN	Parent Case Information	EXA	Assistant Examiner
RLAP	Related US App. Data	REF	Referenced By
REIS	Reissue Data	FREF	Foreign References
PRIR	Foreign Priority	OREF	Other References
PCT	PCT Information	GOVT	Government Interest
APT	Application Type		

In Advanced Search, basically you may search any keywords in any fields and mix any fields in a Boolean combination. In your search query, you define a field and keyword separated by a forward slash. Every field of a patent is represented by a two-letter to four-letter acronym. Fortunately, you do not need to remember these search field acronyms. The list is conveniently provided to you in the same web page as you enter your query, and is illustrated in Table 15.1. All you need to know is the query syntax and how to form Boolean combinations.

The following examples of queries will give you a quick start.

Examples:

1. Tennis and (racquet or racket) – Search for patents with "Tennis and racquet" both appearing in any fields or "Tennis and racket" both appearing in any fields. Note, no fields being defined means searching applies to all fields.
2. ABST/(Tennis and (racquet or racket)) or SPEC/(Tennis and (racquet or racket)) – search for patents with Tennis and (Racquet or racket) both appearing in any of abstract or specification fields.
3. IN/(John and Smith) – search for the words John and Smith both appearing in inventor's name field.
4. IN/("John Smith") – search for patents with John Smith as inventor.
5. CCL/270/$ and AN/"Roll Systems" – search all patents classified as US Class 270 and all subclasses and those assigned to Roll Systems.

Searching Results

The search tool gives you a list of patents that meet your query. You can click on any of the patents in the list to view details of each patent. Each patent is displayed by default in full text in the web browser. The text can be searched by either hitting Ctrl-F or selecting "Find" under "edit" drop down menu of your browser. The text can also be copied and pasted to a third party application.

In addition to text, a patent can be displayed in patent image page should you desire to view drawings. In order to do that, you need to install the adequate TIFF plug-in, and once the plug-in is installed, you can view patent full page images page by page inside the browser. The text displayed in patent image page mode is treated as static image thus cannot be selected or searched.

Searching Tips

Among various types of queries, searching by subject (or keywords) is the most challenging. Like using any search engines (e.g. Google, Yahoo!), you will get better and more efficient when you are experienced in coming up with the right keywords and Boolean combinations, which give you reasonable amount of information without overwhelming you. Searching patents by keywords too, requires trial-and-error. The following lists some tips pertaining to patent search that you may find helpful.

1. Start with some different variations of keywords to see if you are getting any reasonable return: how many are returned and whether most of the returned patents are relevant or too far off. If you get 1000 patents returned, that is too many to be productive reviewing them. If you get 100–300 patents returned, it is feasible to browse each of the patents (at least the titles) and cherry pick what you think may be relevant.

2. Try to use the right truncation feature to cover many variations of a word. For example, if you are searching for something relevant to "video retrieval", you may want to use "video" and "retriev$" ($ is a wildcard) to cover variations such as "retrieve", "retrieving" and "retrieval" as some people may use "retrieving video" instead of "video retrieval".

3. The title of a patent is not normally used in the searching, especially in searching by subject unless you know the exact title. Searching is commonly conducted in abstracts and specification, whereas claims are rarely used for general patent search.

4. To conduct efficient patent search in your targeted genre, you may want to combine your keyword search with U.S. or international patent classification (IPC). If you have already known the general class of your technology field, you may want to use it to limit your search range. Being familiar with patent classification is particularly important if you are doing patent search frequently. For more details on patent classification system, refer to Section 3 of this chapter.

15.1.2　*Google Patent Search*

Google Patent Search (http://www.google.com) was launched towards the end of 2006 and has been enjoyed by many users. It is also a free web-based search tool for US issued patents and published applications. All patents available through Google Patent Search come from the

USPTO. If Google's patent information is originally from the USPTO, why is there a need to use Google Patent Search? Well, Google claims they have integrated a search engine riding on the power of Google Book Search. Google Patent Search is still in Beta version at the time of this writing, and it is still undergoing much improvement. However, Google Patent Search offers several unique features over the USPTO patent database as follows.

1. The display of patents is done through a rich and intuitive graphical user interface, in which some key patent information like title, abstract, and claims is displayed side by side conveniently in one screen. Even you are viewing it on a small laptop screen, such information is properly laid out without being clumsy, as illustrated in Fig. 15.3.

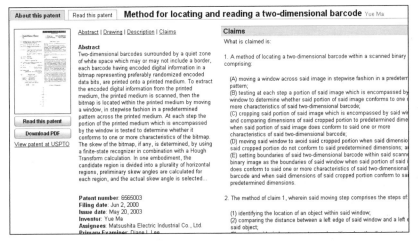

Fig. 15.3 The user interface of Google Patent Search.

2. There is no need to install a plug-in viewer as for the USPTO patent database. The patent image page is also searchable by keywords.
3. Both backward and forward citations are included in the same web page for convenient viewing.
4. Patents are available to download as PDF files.
5. A hyperlink is available for user to directly jump into the USPTO page for the same patent if he so wishes.

In my view, Google Patent Search is better for displaying/browsing patents than searching due to its limited search capabilities being offered at the present time. The USPTO's simple-to-use query language seems to be more powerful for sophisticated patent searchers. Last, if you are particularly interested in patents just issued, Google database may not be up to date as it needs time to integrate new information from the USPTO on a weekly basis.

15.2 International and Other Foreign Patent Databases

Foreign patents can be searched in each country's patent office website. For most non-English speaking countries, there is usually a minimal English interface that allows you to retrieve patent abstract in English. This section will introduce two popular database sites for international patents, namely International patent application database at WIPO and European country patent database at esp@cenet.

15.2.1 *International Patent Database*

An international patent application (PCT application) will be published automatically at the international bureau (i.e. WIPO – World Intellectual Property Office) 18 months after its priority date, which is the filing date of the PCT application unless it claims the priority of another foreign patent. The published PCT applications are available for free public access through WIPO's main website at http://www.wipo.org or directly at http://www.wipo.int/pctdb/en/.

Similar to the USPTO patent database, WIPO patent search (called PatentScope) offers Simple Search and Advanced Search. The Simple Search provides Boolean search combining keywords for different fields, whereas the Advanced Search has quite similar feature to those of the USPTO. The Advanced Search requires user to enter his query that defines field and keywords separated by a forward slash. The field definition is not compatible with that of the USPTO, and it is illustrated in Table. 15.2.

Table 15.2 Search field names for WIPO Advanced Search.

Field Code	Field Name	Example
WO	Publication Number	WO/02/00157 OR WO2002/00158
AN	Application Number	AN/PCT/DE03/01815 OR AN/FR2004/002712
ET	English Title	ET/needle OR ET/syringe
FT	French Title	FT/aiguille OR FT/seringue
JT	Japanese Title	
IC	International Class	IC/H04Q-7/22 OR IC/H04N-*
ABE	English Abstract	ABE/"hypodermic needle" OR ABE/syringe
ABF	French Abstract	ABF/"aiguille hypodermique" or ABF/seringue
ABJ	Japanese Abstract	
DE	Description	DE/needle AND DE/phonograph
CL	Claims	CL/needle OR CL/syringe
FP	Front Page Bibliographic Data	FP/hovercraft
DP	Publication Date	DP/19.02.1998 OR DP/1998.02.19
AD	Application Date	AD/22.10.2004 OR AD/2004.10.23
NP	Priority Number	NP/0312464
PD	Priority Date	PD/24.10.2003 OR PD/2003.10.25
PCN	Priority Country	PCN/FR
DS	Designated States	DS/US AND DS/DE
IN	Inventor Name	IN/"Smith, John"
IAD	Inventor Address	IAD/Seattle
PA	Applicant Name	PA/"General Mot*" or PA/Ford
AAD	Applicant Address	AAD/Paris NEAR AAD/TX
ARE	Applicant Residence	ARE/US
ANA	Applicant Nationality	ANA/GB
RP	Legal Rep. Name	RP/"Jones, Will*"
RAD	Legal Rep. Address	RAD/Bellevue
RCN	Legal Rep. Country	RCN/DE
LGP	Language of Pub.	LGP/DE or LGP/JA
LGF	Language of Filing	LGF/EN OR LGF/FR
ICI	International Class (inventive)	ICI/F02M-45/08 OR ICI/A61N-*

Table 15.2 (Continued)

Field Code	Field Name	Example
ICN	International Class (noninventive)	ICN/F02M-45/08 OR ICN/A61N-*
NPCC	National Phase Country Code	NPCC/AU
NPED	National Phase Entry Date	NPED/20060101->20061231
NPAN	National Phase Application Number	NPAN/11003666
NPET	National Phase Entry Type	NPET/C

The retrieved results from WIPO search give you the detailed bibliographical data of each patent as well as description and claims in full text. In addition, the system also shows up-to-date status of each application (e.g. national phase and notices) and makes related documents available for download in a bundled ZIP file of TIFF images or a single multi-page PDF file. These related documents include original patent application, written opinion of the International Search Authority, or International Preliminary Report on Patentability and International Search Report.

The WIPO international application database offers a powerful tool for fulfilling many searching needs. In comparison to the USPTO database, WIPO database has the following unique features:

1. Richer query syntax with added proximity feature that allows searcher to define two words appearing in the text within proximity (e.g. five words, for example) of each other.
2. Free user account that maintains your last 20 search sessions.
3. All documents are available in PDF files.
4. Statistics of your search results gives you indication of the effectiveness of your search per keyword. A keyword that generates too many returns may not be effective. For example, a search using keywords video and compression in English titles gives the following statistics:

    ET/video: 8282 occurrences in 7540 records.

    ET/compression: 2775 occurrences in 266

    (ET/video AND ET/compression): 204 records.

Therefore, you would never want to use keyword "video" alone in your search.

The limitation of WIPO database is that it only contains PCT published applications.

15.2.2 *European Patent Database*

Another popular free database is esp@cenet (pronounced as E-SPACE-NET) sponsored by European Patent Office and is available at http://ep.espacenet.com. It contains over 60 million patent documents from all over the world including all WIPO PCT applications, European patents as well as patents from worldwide covering 85 countries.

The idea of esp@cenet project was to concentrate more on patent application publications than on granted patents for the reason that patent applications are usually the first publications appearing before journal articles are published or products entering into the market. For this reason, WIPO PCT applications are completely covered in esp@cenet.

Like all other patent databases, esp@cenet's search capability includes the Quick Search and Advanced Search. The Advanced Search is still graphical user interface driven instead of using a query language; therefore, it does not offer nearly sophisticated searching options as USPTO or WIPO does. The unique features of esp@cenet are listed as below.

Patent Family Information

Once you find a patent in one country, it will also tell you if the same invention has been filed in other countries. The patent family information is very important for patent licensing and sales, in which case the perspective licensee or buyer would want to know whether they are acquiring any corresponding legal rights in other countries besides the home country.

Figure 15.4 shows that a complete list of patent family members can be retrieved by user clicking on "View INPADOC patent family" hyperlink, or any individual country patent document (publication or granted patent) can be downloaded or viewed.

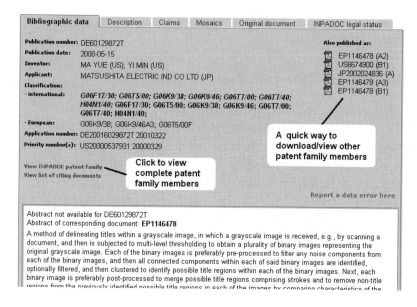

Fig. 15.4 Patent family members view.

Legal Status Information

For each country the esp@cenet interface shows the status of each application by user clicking "INPADOC legal status" tab, as shown in the upper right corner of Fig. 15.4.

If you are interested in PCT applications, European or other country patents, esp@cenet is the best place to meet your patent search needs. Like most other patent database tools, a PDF copy of a patent is available for download.

15.3   Patent Classification

Patent Classification is a codified system for categorizing an invention. The classification is used both as a tool for finding patents, and for assisting in the assignment of patent applications to examiners. For patent search purposes, patent classification is a powerful tool and can be a good complement to keyword search. If you are an expert in a particular technology domain, it is strongly advised that you familiarize yourself with the patent classification system and find the class(es) that cover your domain. These patent classes will come handy for your future patent search.

As you may notice in Chapter 4, a patent cover page includes both U.S. Class and International Patent Class (IPC) codes. These are firstly assigned at the USPTO before the patent examination begins. Each U.S. patent will receive at least one or more classifications assigned to it. The U.S. Class and IPC are different classification systems. The U.S. Class is defined by the USPTO while the IPC is administrated by the WIPO. These two systems are not compatible although much effort has been made within the USPTO on the mapping between the two.

15.3.1 *U.S. Patent Classification*

The U.S. classification is typically expressed as "class/subclass" e.g. "704/1". The first number, 704, represents the class of invention. The number following the forward slash is the subclass of invention within the class. There are about 450 classes and about 150,000 subclasses of invention in the U.S. patent classification system.

Figure 15.5 shows the U.S. classification hierarchy for class 704. Under this class, the subclass contains numeric value with or without dots. For example, Class 704/200.1 is defined as psychoacoustic technologies for speech, linguistics, language translation or audio compression related data processing. Further, the subclass definition shows various indent levels as indicated by one or multiple dots, whereas the mainline (without dots) is considered as the highest level. In this example, the highest level subclasses of 704 are: 704/1, 704/200, as well as 704/500 and 704/503 (now shown).

To familiarize yourself with the patent classification system, the best resource is the USPTO website, where you can find numerous tools and documents[1]. Among the tools available at the USPTO, two are frequently used and are listed as follows:

1. Manual of Classification (MOC). It is an ordered listing of all the valid classifications which are presented as class schedules as shown in Fig. 15.5. Class schedules are arranged in the numerical order for both class and subclass levels.

```
CLASS 704 DATA PROCESSING: SPEECH SIGNAL PROCESSING,
LINGUISTICS, LANGUAGE TRANSLATION, AND AUDIO
COMPRESSION/DECOMPRESSION

1        LINGUISTICS
2        .Translation machine
3        ..Having particular Input/Output device
4        ..Based on phrase, clause, or idiom
5        ..For partial translation
6        ..Punctuation
7        ..Storage or retrieval of data
8        .Multilingual or national language support
9        .Natural language
10       .Dictionary building, modification, or
         prioritization
200      SPEECH SIGNAL PROCESSING
200.1    .Psychoacoustic
201      .For storage or transmission
202      ..Neural network
         ...
```

Fig. 15.5 Example of U.S. classification hierarchy.

2. Classification Index. It is an index to the classification system or the Manual of Classification (MOC). It lists technical subject matter alphabetically using ordinary terminology and directs user to the general area of the MOC listing subclasses related to that subject matter.

A common task associated with patent classification is to first identify the relevant classification pertaining to your invention. The combined use of the two aforementioned tools will help you accomplish this task. Let us take a look at the following example.

---

[1] http://www.uspto.gov/web/offices/opc/documents/overview.pdf.

Example

Suppose the invention we need to classify is an air circulation device that uses a window opening to draw cold air in from outside and vent out warm air from inside the house. It is designed to improve the efficiency of air ventilation therefore reduce the up time of air conditioning system. The goal is to find relevant classifications. The key features of the invention include: ventilation fan, automatic control, portable and attachable to a window. The exclusions are: no heating (limited to air cooling only), no heat exchange unit, no fluid or agent materials.

The first step is to use the Classification Index to find related classification to the subject matter. Using the keywords "air" and "fan", we found the following candidate classes:

Air
- circulating air: 237/12.3A
- air conditioning equipment: D23/351
- auto cooling and heating: 165/201

Fan
- ventilation: 454

The second step is to fine tune these classifications using the MOC table. By looking at MOC, we found that class for 237 is HEATING SYSTEMS. Clearly, without looking further at its subclasses, we can eliminate 237/12.3A because the invention is not a heating system.

Furthermore, the class D23 is for design patents; therefore is eliminated from our interest.

The class schedule for 165/201 shows 165 HEATING EXCHANGE. Because the invention does not cover heat exchange, class 165/201 is removed.

Finally, from reviewing of the class schedule of 454, related classes are shown below:

454 VENTILATION
195 **MEANS COMBINED WITH DOOR**
196 **MEANS COMBINED WITH WINDOW**
200 . With air pump
201 .. Cooling air conditioner

205   .. Recirculation means
208   .. Propeller fan having rotary axis perpendicular to window
211   . Having air passage in sash
214   . Having air passage between sill and bottom of sash
237   **HAVING BOTH INLET AND OUTLET AIRWAYS**
239   . Including automatic control means
241   . Including unitary inlet and outlet housing
242   .. Rooftop
243   .. Sleeved vent for ceiling, wall or floor (e.g. thimble)
249   .. With air pump
251   . With air pump means
252   .. For both inlet and outlet airways
253   .. For outlet airway
254   **HAVING INLET AIRWAY**
339   **HAVING OUTLET AIRWAY**

From the mainline level (i.e. bold font without indented dots), subclasses 196, 237 seem to be relevant. Further scanning of subclass 196 to the next sublevel shows 200 and 214 relevant. The scanning of subclass 200 at two-dot level further shows both 205 and 208 relevant. Therefore, deriving from subclass 196, we have selected 205, 208 and 214. Under 237, at the first-dot level, 239, 241 and 251 are relevant. Scanning at two-dot level further shows 249, 252 and 253 relevant. Therefore, deriving from subclass 237, we have selected 239, 249 and 251 as 251 covers both 252 and 253.

The final list of relevant classifications is: 454/205, 454/208, 454/214, 454/239, 454/249 and 454/251.

15.3.2 *International Patent Classification*

The International Patent Classification (IPC) is defined in a hierarchy consisting of one, three and four digits, respectively. The IPC also defines a numerical subclass under each four digit classification. An example is shown in Fig. 15.6.

H — ELECTRICITY
H02 — ELECTRIC COMMUNICATION TECHNIQUE
  H04B — BROADCAST COMMUNICATION
    1/00 **Broadcast distribution systems**
    1/02 . Wired systems
    1/04 . . using carrier waves
    1/06 . . . having frequencies in two or more frequency bands
    1/08 . . . combined with telephone network over which...
    1/10 . . using signals not modulated on a carrier
    1/12 . . . not sharing the network with any other service
    1/14 . . combined with power distribution network

    3/00 **Common-wave systems..**
     . . .

Fig. 15.6 Example of International Patent Classification (IPC) hierarchy.

As can be seen, the IPC system consists of 4 levels of hierarchical classifications: 1-digit, 3-digit, 4-digit and numerical values, respectively. Table 15.3 only lists the 1-digit and some exemplary 3-digit and 4-digit classes whereas the entire list of IPC classes can be found online at WIPO website.

In the IPC system, the 1-digit level of IPC has only 8 classes from A to H. The second level uses 3 digits to define less than 150 classes. To count all 1-digit, 3-digit and 4-digit levels, there are approximately 800 classes. The total number of subclasses under 4-digit level is about 69,000. In comparison, the IPC seems to have significant fewer number of classes in total ($<$50%) than that of the U.S. classification system.

Table 15.3 List of 1-digit and exemplary 3-digit and 4-digit IPC classes.

Class	Class Definition
A	**A — HUMAN NECESSITIES**
B	**B — PERFORMING OPERATIONS; TRANSPORTING**
C	**C — CHEMISTRY; METALLURGY**
D	**D — TEXTILES; PAPER**
E	**E — FIXED CONSTRUCTIONS**

Table 15.3 (Continued)

Class	Class Definition
F	**F — MECHANICAL ENGINEERING; LIGHTING; HEATING; WEAPONS; BLASTING**
G	**G — PHYSICS**
...	...
G06	COMPUTING; CALCULATING; COUNTING (score computers for games Fulltext...
G06C	DIGITAL COMPUTERS IN WHICH ALL THE COMPUTATION IS EFFECTED MECHANICALLY (score computers for card games Fulltext...
G06D	DIGITAL FLUID-PRESSURE COMPUTING DEVICES
G06E	OPTICAL COMPUTING DEVICES (optical logic elements per se Fulltext...
G06F	ELECTRIC DIGITAL DATA PROCESSING (computers in which a part of the computation is effected hydraulically or pneumatically Fulltext...
G06G	ANALOGUE COMPUTERS (analogue optical computing devices Fulltext...
G06J	HYBRID COMPUTING ARRANGEMENTS (optical hybrid computing devices Fulltext...
G06K	RECOGNITION OF DATA; PRESENTATION OF DATA; RECORD CARRIERS; HANDLING RECORD CARRIERS (postal sorting Fulltext...
.....	.....
H	**H — ELECTRICITY**
H01	BASIC ELECTRIC ELEMENTS
H02	GENERATION, CONVERSION, OR DISTRIBUTION OF ELECTRIC POWER
H03	BASIC ELECTRONIC CIRCUITRY
H04	ELECTRIC COMMUNICATION TECHNIQUE
H05	ELECTRIC TECHNIQUES NOT OTHERWISE PROVIDED FOR
H99	SUBJECT MATTER NOT OTHERWISE PROVIDED FOR IN THIS SECTION [8]

15.3.3 *Concordance to International Patent Classification*

The USPTO provides the mapping of each of U.S. classification for utility patents to the corresponding IPC. Given any U.S. classification, a user can easily look up its IPC code via the online classification definition tool and select "US-to-IPC8 Concordance", as shown in Fig. 15.7. A PDF version concordance table for the example shown is also available at USPTO website[2].

---

[2] http://www.uspto.gov/go/classification/conpdf/us_con_454.pdf.

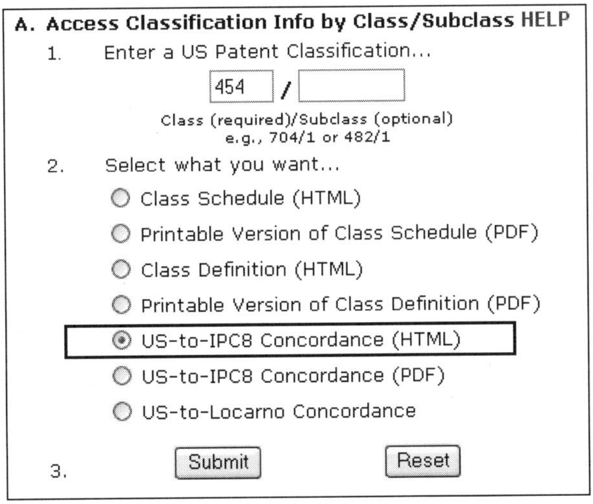

A. Access Classification Info by Class/Subclass HELP

1.   Enter a US Patent Classification...

                 454   /   [   ]

          Class (required)/Subclass (optional)
              e.g., 704/1 or 482/1

2.   Select what you want...

   ○ Class Schedule (HTML)
   ○ Printable Version of Class Schedule (PDF)
   ○ Class Definition (HTML)
   ○ Printable Version of Class Definition (PDF)
   ◉ US-to-IPC8 Concordance (HTML)
   ○ US-to-IPC8 Concordance (PDF)
   ○ US-to-Locarno Concordance

3.   [Submit]   [Reset]

Fig. 15.7 U.S. classification to IPC concordance.

15.4   Progressive Patent Search

Each week on Tuesdays, the USPTO publishes newly issued patents as well as new patent applications; therefore, thousands of new entries are added to the patent database each week. Depending on your patent search tasks, you may need to conduct similar search progressively on a weekly or monthly basis to include all up-to-date patents and publications.

15.4.1 *Saving Search Terms*

In order to save any repetitive work, the best way is to save your search session or search terms every time you conduct your search. Saving your search terms is also a good working protocol in doing any patent search, for which your session can be restored either by yourself or someone else. The benefit of saving your patent search terms is huge in the long run.

Patent Search Report

Search Date: 2/10/2004
Search Terms: (USPTO query used)

(cls/348$ or cls/725$) and (VOD or "video on demand")

Search Results after triage (list of patents and simple remark):

1. 6,647,411 Intel, Secure cached subscription service (Note: allows video contents to be downloaded through computer network based on user's data at cached device)
2. 6,684,400 Diva system, Method and apparatus for providing dynamic pricing services for an interactive information distribution system (Note: package pricing model for subscription-on-demand. Dynamic GUI mechanism between head-end and STB to offer more than video store experience at inexpensive cost at STB)
3. 6,658,663, Philips, Business model for leasing storage on digital recorder (Note: local HDD storage space on STB is controlled remotely by the MSO, and different pricing is associated with upgrading storage space).
4. 6,438,596, Toshiba, Video on demand system that presents users with a selection list of proposed videos for which server and network resources are available to immediately serve the selected video (Note: present a list of programs based on the probability that it is immediately available on the server and network

Fig. 15.8 A sample patent search report.

Figure 15.8 shows a sample of a simple patent search report. In addition to the list of related patents found, the date of the search and the query being used in the search are also included in the report. This stored information allows a user to accomplish a few other tasks easily, as described in the following exemplary scenarios.

1. <u>To restore/modify a search</u>. Suppose you submitted your patent disclosure along with a preliminary search report. The corporate patent committee is trying to decide whether to file the disclosure and wants a review on the IP situation of neighboring technologies. You or someone can copy/paste the previous search terms and modify only one or two keywords and plug into the USPTO Advanced Search page to see how many patents are returned. The task can be easily accomplished without having to construct the query from scratch.

2. <u>To update a search with new patents and publications</u>. Suppose you conducted a preliminary search when you first conceived the idea. Six months later, you have worked out all the details of the invention and are ready to file your patent. You want to run another search just to make sure there are no other patents or publications showing up during these six months that covers your invention. To do this, you can simply copy/paste your previous query, and modify the starting date to when you did your preliminary search. In that way, you are only searching through new patents published since your last search.

3. <u>To monitor the market and IP trend</u>. Suppose you are responsible for watching emerging competitors or innovations in relation to your company's flagship product. You have developed a set of search terms in relation to the underlying technologies employed in the product and generated a preliminary search report. Your company's product is selling well in the market. However, your effort on the monitoring of competitors should continue and you need to repetitively conduct similar patent search periodically, e.g. monthly or bi-monthly. This can be easily done by using the same search term and only expanding your date range every time you do the patent search.

As previously described, both USPTO and WIPO give you advanced search capability that allow you to enter script like query terms in text. Your query terms can be saved, copied/pasted to your search report easily. In addition, if you are using WIPO and sign up for a free account, you can save your search session and resume later.

15.4.2 *Monitoring Fresh Patents*

A useful web based tool called freshpatents.com can be found at: http://www.freshpatents.com/. It gives you a weekly update on newly published patent applications from the USPTO. The delay is about four to five days. Freshpatents.com is not a great place to search for patent publications. Rather, it is a great monitoring and tracking tool. Here is a highlight of freshpatents.com features.

1. Browsing. Patent applications can be browsed by popular categories, popular companies, inventor names or attorney/agent names. Listed patents are grouped either by publication date or by month.
2. Monitoring and Tracking. You may sign up for a free account and set your keywords for tracking. The keywords are to be applied to all fields including title, abstract, inventor names, and patent attorney/agent names. Every week when new patent applications become available, any new applications that match your keywords will be sent to you by email.
3. Organizing. If you browse online, you may save your viewed patents for later review. You may also track previous monitoring emails that have been sent to you.

What about privacy? The website only asks you minimal information in order to sign you up, but as with any online account you sign up, you should always be prudent with what information you give out and what kind of keywords you are using that may reveal the nature of your own business.

15.5   USPTO PAIR and Image File Wrapper

People may not realize that the USPTO website is not only a place to search patents, but also a place to find out the status of any patent or application and retrieve related documents. The gateway to this additional information and documents is Patent Application Information Retrieval (PAIR) and Patent eBusiness, which can be accessed through USPTO website or directly at http://portal.uspto.gov/external/portal/pair.

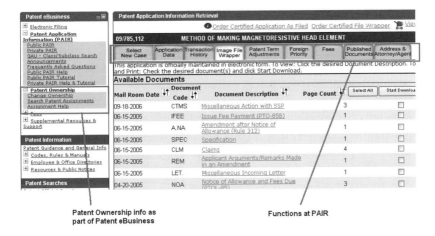

Patent Ownership info as
part of Patent eBusiness

Functions at PAIR

Fig. 15.9 Patent eBusiness and PAIR available at USPTO.

There are two versions of PAIR: public PAIR and private PAIR. Public PAIR provides status and history information for issued patents and published applications to the general public with unrestricted access. Public PAIR also provides access to the image file wrapper (IFW, to be explained below) for online viewing and downloading. Private PAIR allows independent inventors and registered practitioners such as attorneys or agents to access real-time status of their pending patent applications.

A snapshot of PAIR and Patent eBusiness page is shown in Fig. 15.9. The highlights of functions at PAIR and Patent eBusiness are:

1. Application data. It gives you the status information about a patent or patent application, examiner's name, USPTO group art unit handling the examination, filing date, publication date, application number, U.S. class, inventor's name etc.
2. Transaction history. It gives you a list of transactions associated with the patent application or issued patent such as filing date, Office Action and response date, notice of allowance, issue date etc.
3. Image File Wrapper (IFW). IFW contains all related documents generated during a patent prosecution. These documents in the file wrapper can either be displayed online in an image viewer or bundled in PDF. For applications filed after 2003, the prosecution history

should be automatically available in the file wrapper in the public PAIR.

4. Maintenance fee. You can check each payment window when maintenance fee is due for 3 ½, 7 ½ and 11 ½ year and the status of payment or lapse if the patent owner failed to pay.

5. Patent ownership. You may check the assignment record and any transfer of ownership, if any, during the life of the patent. Although not required by law, it is a common practice that if the patent owner sells the patent, the original or true copy of the new assignment should be submitted for recordation with the USPTO. Other types of documents commonly recorded by the PTO include mergers, changes of business names etc. Any recorded documents will be available in the patent ownership service. This service is in fact part of Patent eBusiness and can be accessed from PAIR web page.

To conclude, there is abundant information available at the USPTO PAIR. Familiarize yourself with the system and use it as a source for checking your application status or due diligence associated with any patent evaluation activity. You may find information more timely than you would from your company's outside patent attorney or paralegal support.

Patent Country Code

The patent country code, also referred to as the WIPO Standard ST.3, has been codified and in force by the WIPO since 1978. The standard provides two-letter alphabetic codes for the purpose of improving the access to patent information particularly those requiring identifying the country of issuance. It is intended to be implemented for any use by intellectual property offices requiring the identification of countries in coded form. In practice, the patent country codes come handy and have been widely used in patent databases in representing either an individual patent or a family of counter parts belonging to different countries. A list of country code is shown in Table A-1.

Table A-1 List of patent country code.

Code	Country	Code	Country
AD	Andorra	KM	Comoros
AE	United Arab Emirates	KN	Saint Kitts and Nevis
AF	Afghanistan	KP	Democratic People's Republic of Korea
AG	Antigua and Barbuda	KR	Republic of Korea
AI	Anguilla	KW	Kuwait
AL	Albania	KY	Cayman Islands
AM	Armenia	KZ	Kazakhstan
AN	Netherlands Antilles	LA	Lao People's Democratic Republic
AO	Angola	LB	Lebanon
AP	African Regional Intellectual Property Organization (ARIPO)	LC	Saint Lucia

Table A-1 (Continued)

Code	Country	Code	Country
AR	Argentina	LI	Liechtenstein
AT	Austria	LK	Sri Lanka
AU	Australia	LR	Liberia
AW	Aruba	LS	Lesotho
AZ	Azerbaijan	LT	Lithuania
BA	Bosnia and Herzegovina	LU	Luxembourg
BB	Barbados	LV	Latvia
BD	Bangladesh	LY	Libyan Arab Jamahiriya
BE	Belgium	MA	Morocco
BF	Burkina Faso	MC	Monaco
BG	Bulgaria	MD	Republic of Moldova
BH	Bahrain	ME	Montenegro
BI	Burundi	MG	Madagascar
BJ	Benin	MK	The former Yugoslav Republic of Macedonia
BM	Bermuda	ML	Mali
BN	Brunei Darussalam	MM	Myanmar
BO	Bolivia	MN	Mongolia
BR	Brazil	MO	Macao
BS	Bahamas	MP	Northern Mariana Islands
BT	Bhutan	MR	Mauritania
BV	Bouvet Island	MS	Montserrat
BW	Botswana	MT	Malta
BX	Benelux Office for Intellectual Property (BOIP)	MU	Mauritius
BY	Belarus	MV	Maldives
BZ	Belize	MW	Malawi
CA	Canada	MX	Mexico
CD	Democratic Republic of the Congo	MY	Malaysia
CF	Central African Republic	MZ	Mozambique
CG	Congo	NA	Namibia
CH	Switzerland	NE	Niger
CI	Côte d'Ivoire	NG	Nigeria
CK	Cook Islands	NI	Nicaragua
CL	Chile	NL	Netherlands
CM	Cameroon	NO	Norway

Table A-1 (Continued)

Code	Country	Code	Country
CN	China	NP	Nepal
CO	Colombia	NR	Nauru
CR	Costa Rica	NZ	New Zealand
CU	Cuba	OA	African Intellectual Property Organization (OAPI)
CV	Cape Verde	OM	Oman
CY	Cyprus	PA	Panama
CZ	Czech Republic	PE	Peru
DE	Germany	PG	Papua New Guinea
DJ	Djibouti	PH	Philippines
DK	Denmark	PK	Pakistan
DM	Dominica	PL	Poland
DO	Dominican Republic	PT	Portugal
DZ	Algeria	PW	Palau
EA	Eurasian Patent Organization (EAPO)	PY	Paraguay
EC	Ecuador	QA	Qatar
EE	Estonia	QZ	Community Plant Variety Office (European Community) (CPVO)
EG	Egypt	RO	Romania
EH	Western Sahara	RS	Serbia
EM	Office for Harmonization in the Internal Market (Trademarks and Designs) (OHIM)	RU	Russian Federation
EP	European Patent Office (EPO)	RW	Rwanda
ER	Eritrea	SA	Saudi Arabia
ES	Spain	SB	Solomon Islands
ET	Ethiopia	SC	Seychelles
FI	Finland	SD	Sudan
FJ	Fiji	SE	Sweden
FK	Falkland Islands (Malvinas)	SG	Singapore
FO	Faroe Islands	SH	Saint Helena
FR	France	SI	Slovenia
GA	Gabon	SK	Slovakia
GB	United Kingdom	SL	Sierra Leone

Table A-1 (Continued)

Code	Country	Code	Country
GC	Patent Office of the Cooperation Council for the Arab States of the Gulf (GCC)	SM	San Marino
GD	Grenada	SN	Senegal
GE	Georgia	SO	Somalia
GG	Guernsey	SR	Suriname
GH	Ghana	ST	Sao Tome and Principe
GI	Gibraltar	SV	El Salvador
GL	Greenland	SY	Syrian Arab Republic
GM	Gambia	SZ	Swaziland
GN	Guinea	TC	Turks and Caicos Islands
GQ	Equatorial Guinea	TD	Chad
GR	Greece	TG	Togo
GS	South Georgia and the South Sandwich Islands	TH	Thailand
GT	Guatemala	TJ	Tajikistan
GW	Guinea-Bissau	TL	Timor–Leste
GY	Guyana	TM	Turkmenistan
HK	The Hong Kong Special Administrative Region of the People's Republic of China	TN	Tunisia
HN	Honduras	TO	Tonga
HR	Croatia	TR	Turkey
HT	Haiti	TT	Trinidad and Tobago
HU	Hungary	TV	Tuvalu
IB	International Bureau of the World Intellectual Property Organization (WIPO)(4)	TW	Taiwan, Province of China
ID	Indonesia	TZ	United Republic of Tanzania
IE	Ireland	UA	Ukraine
IL	Israel	UG	Uganda
IM	Isle of Man	US	United States of America
IN	India	UY	Uruguay
IQ	Iraq	UZ	Uzbekistan WS Samoa
IR	Iran (Islamic Republic of)	VA	Holy See XN Nordic Patent Institute (NPI)
IS	Iceland	VC	Saint Vincent and the Grenadines
IT	Italy	VE	Venezuela

Table A-1 (Continued)

Code	Country	Code	Country
JE	Jersey	YE	Yemen
JM	Jamaica	VG	Virgin Islands (British)
JO	Jordan	VN	Viet Nam
JP	Japan	VU	Vanuatu
KE	Kenya	ZA	South Africa
KG	Kyrgyzstan	ZM	Zambia
KH	Cambodia	ZW	Zimbabwe
KI	Kiribati	WO	World Intellectual Property Organization (WIPO) (International Bureau of)(4)

Appendix B

Patent Kind Code

The WIPO has standardized the patent kind code, referred to as Standard ST.16, to serve the purpose of distinguishing patent documents published by intellectual property offices.

The ST.16 standard defines the kind code as one letter code, followed by one-digit numerical code, if necessary, to supplement the information contained in the letter code. The ST.16 specifies seven groups of codes to use for different types of patents. For example, Group 1 is used for documents resulting from a patent application and being identified as the primary or major series. It contains three letter codes: A, B and C to represent the first, second and third publication levels, respectively. A complete document describing ST.16 kind code can be found at the WIPO's website[1].

The ST.16 standard establishes basic letter codes and numerical codes while providing some flexibility for each country's intellectual property office according to its needs. In fact, in order to interpret kind code appearing in any country's patent document, one needs to look up in that particular country's kind code definition. For example, Table B-1 lists the kind codes for U.S. patents following the WIPO ST.16 standard as of January 2, 2001.

---

[1] http://www.wipo.int/standards/en/pdf/03-16-01.pdf.

Table B-1 Definition of new U.S. patent kind code after January 2, 2001.

WIPO ST.16 Kind Codes	Kind of document	Comments
A1	Patent Application Publication	
A2	Patent Application Publication (Republication)	
A9	Patent Application Publication (Corrected Publication)	
B1	Patent	No previously published pre-grant publication
B2	Patent	Having a previously published pre-grant publication
C1, C2, C3...	Reexamination Certificate	Previously used codes B1 and B2 are now used for granted patents
E	Reissue Patent	
H	Statutory Invention Registration (SIR)	
P1	Plant Patent Application Publication	
P2	Plant Patent	No previously published pre-grant publication
P3	Plant Patent	Having a previously published pre-grant publication
P4	Plant Patent Application Publication (Republication)	
P9	Plant Patent Application Publication (Corrected Publication)	
S	Design Patent	

Before January 2, 2001, the USPTO was using a different kind code notation. If you are reading a patent published before January 2, 2001, you may refer to the kind code as shown in Table B-2.

Table B-2 Definition of U.S. patent kind code before January 2, 2001.

WIPO ST.16 Kind Codes	Kind of document	Comments
A	Patent	Kind code replaced by B1 or B2
P	Plant Patent	Kind code replaced by P2 or P3
B1, B2, B3...	Reexamination Certificate	Kind code replaced by C1, C2, C3...

References

Anson, W. and Suchy, D. (editors), Intellectual Property Valuation, The American Bar Association, 2005.

Berman, B. (editor), From Ideas to Assets, Wiley, 2002.

Burge, D., Patent and Trademark Tactics and Practices, 3rd ed, Wiley, 1999.

Charmasson, H., Patents, Copyrights and Trademarks for Dummies, Wiley, 2000.

Emma, P., Patents: To File or Not to File? *IEEE Micro*, September-October, pp. 79-81, 2005.

Emma, P., Prosecuting Your Patent, *IEEE Micro*, September-October, pp. 87-88, 2006.

Fox, D.L., Product-By-Process Claims: A Possible Answer Under Phillips to the Atlantic – Scripps Schism, *Intellectual Property Today*, pp. 33-37, Oct. 2006.

Hershkowitz, B., What Are My Chances? From Idea Through Litigation, http://library.findlaw.com, 2003.

Knight, H.J., Patent Strategy for Researchers and Research Managers, 2nd ed, Wiley, 2006.

Lechter, M.A. (editor), Successful Patents and Patenting for Engineers and Scientist, IEEE Press, 1995.

Malackowski, J. and Barney, J.A., What Is Patent Quality? – A Merchant Banc's Perspective, Colloquium on a Comprehensive Approach to Patent Quality Federation Internationale Des Conseils En propriete Industrielle, Amsterdam, June 8-9, 2007.

Pohl, M., Patent Landscaping Studies: Their Use in Strategic Research Planning, *Pharmaceutical News*, vol. 9, pp. 127-135, 2002.

Poltorak, A.I. and Lerner, P.J., Essentials of Licensing Intellectual Property, Wiley, 2004.

Pressman, D., Patent It Yourself, 12th ed, NOLO, 2006.

Schechter, R.E. and Thomas, J.R., Principles of Patent Law, 2nd ed, Thomson West, 2004.

Stern, R.H., Licensing IP Embodied in Standards, *IEEE Micro*, July-August, pp. 7,8,82,83, 1999.

Stern, R.H., Licensing IP Embodied in Standards Part 2, *IEEE Micro*, September-October, pp. 7-9, 82-83, 1999.

Stern, R.H., Collecting Patent Infringement Damages on Unpatented Products, *IEEE Micro*, May-June, pp. 6-7, 2004.

Stim, R. and Pressman, D., Patent Pending in 24 Hours, 3rd ed. NOLO, 2004.

Stim, R., Patent, Copyright & Trademark, NOLO, 8th ed, 2006.

Stobbs, G., Software Patents, 2nd ed, Aspen and Law Business, 2000.

Index